BUILDING
RELATIONSHIPS
THAT LAST
A LIFETIME

Donna,
[signature]

BUILDING
RELATIONSHIPS
THAT LAST
A LIFETIME

RON
RICE

How to Flourish in Life by Putting People First

credo
house publishers

Building Relationships That Last a Lifetime
Copyright © 2012 by Ron Rice
All rights reserved.

Published in the United States by Credo House Publishers,
a division of Credo Communications, LLC, Grand Rapids, Michigan.
www.credohousepublishers.com

ISBN: 978-1-935391-65-4

Cover design by Melinda Taylor, AREA203 Digital
Interior design and composition by Brian Fowler, DesignTeam
Editorial by Paul Brinkerhoff, Grace and Truth Communications, LLC;
Donna Huisjen; Michael Vander Klipp

Printed in the United States of America

First Edition

Dedicated To **My Three Fathers:**

My Dad, **Ron Rice, Sr.,** for his example
My Father-in-Law, **Len Simons,** for his encouragement
My **Heavenly Father,** for his infinite love

CONTENTS

The Love of Connecting People and Ideas

Researchers tell us that the publishing industry will produce over twenty-five thousand books this year. Do the math and that equals almost seventy books per day. That's seventy completed works, seven days a week, including holidays!

And yet, I've chosen to write a book to add to that staggering number already on the market. Why would I do that? Because I believe I have something to say that you need to hear.

This book is a collection of my thirty years of professional experience and a good deal of personal mistakes and tragedy combined with a little gumption and chutzpah. These ideas, rules, and a few suggestions made me a multimillionaire by my thirty-fifth birthday, and allowed me to retire comfortably at the age of forty-two.

In retirement, I've stayed busy continuing to speak and coach relationship builders at all levels. From a bright-eyed high school graduate to a gray beard veteran of many corporate victories, all have benefited from my no-nonsense approach to understanding and building relationships in all walks of life.

Even today, the key to my success . . . and yours . . . is our ability to locate, develop, grow, and maintain relationships. I've made literally thousands of personal connections that have furthered hundreds of businesses and charitable organizations around the world, and all by simply introducing one relationship to another.

The principals you'll read about in this book have been the backbone of everything I do on a daily basis to achieve success. Many of my routines and activities are common sense to most professional relationship builders, but it is amazing how we all need to hear "the classics" every now and then to keep them fresh and alive in our daily lives. If you will give me a few hours of your time, this book will show everyone something new to add to their professional and personal relationship building objectives.

Since my childhood, I've always enjoyed being around people, and even at the ripe old age of fifty-two, I still hate being alone. Give me interesting people and a good conversation, and you have made my day. The meeting can be with a close family member, or a complete stranger it makes no difference to me. I love the exchange of ideas and goals of each individual's story. People are fascinating if we will only take the time to listen, and then act on what we have just heard *before* we forget it!

Once I've connected with an individual, my mind starts a process of matching what I've learned with what I know about someone or something else. It may be a job or business opportunity, a civic or church activity, or simply a social event that fits someone's interests or objectives. I love making the connection and watching what happens next.

It is a rewarding activity to see others benefit from spending time with you. For me the challenge of sharing enough in people's lives to make a difference gives me great satisfaction and helped me earn a fantastic living by simply connecting people and mutual interests.

I love to talk with professionals about what makes their company strong. Corporate strength comes from developing and growing relationships at all levels. From recruiting, hiring, and developing great people, to locating and building lifelong relationships with clients. Everything positive in our professional lives is based on the relationships we develop and grow . . . and then on our ability to connect those relationships with others.

The same holds true of our personal and family relationships. They must be considered an important investment of our time and effort if they are to survive. Neglect them, and they die.

People often ask me if I miss the day-to-day action of running my own company. The answer is no, because I never really stopped doing what I loved when I ran my own company. Getting to know people and connecting them with something of value as a team is the key to building any great company. Being a boss or owner was not the driving force of my career; it was working with people who share the same vision, work a common plan, and profit from the venture as a whole that made the entire effort worthwhile.

Whether a person is a high-profile Fortune 500 client or a bright-eyed college student wanting to launch a first new idea, all of my relationships had something to teach me just as they do anyone who takes the time to listen and then act on the information. Every relationship we develop bears fruit somewhere in our lives no matter how large or small. We just need to do the work that allows the tree to grow and then enjoy the "fruits" of our labors!

Talking with interesting people was always fun for me. I loved thinking how exciting it would be if that person could meet another contact of mine with the same passion or plan. It still drives my wife, Erin, a little crazy that I'm always looking to "connect" someone. Many of my "matches" have built major corporations, while others just became good friends. Either way, I love it, and will continue to match people and interests for the rest of my life.

One of the gentlemen who edited this book happens to be yet another example of making a connection that benefited both of us. My editor, Mike Vander Klipp has a great idea to promote fathering around the world with a powerful symbol for all dads to wear—a father ring. This simple band worn on a dad's right hand will remind him every day of his children, just like his wedding band reminds him of his commitment to his wife.

Mike contacted me through another friend of a friend because he heard of my work with the National Center for Fathering. Having spent several years on the executive board of this awesome organization that promotes fathering through training and support materials, I knew the contacts Mike would need to launch his idea. After an exchange of business plans and a few brief conversations, I invited Mike to come to Chicago and hear me speak and meet some of my contacts in the fathering movement who were in town that week for meetings. The lunch brought together a commercial jeweler, two executives from the fathering movement, and two entrepreneurs who had built several organizations from scratch. Everyone loved the idea and agreed to several action steps to move the plan forward. Mike left the lunch with pages of ideas and action steps.

After the meeting, Mike asked me if there was anything he could do to help me with any projects or ideas I was working on. I mentioned to him that I was finishing a book on relationships and trying to navigate my way in the wide world of publishing. Did I mention already that Mike is an experienced book editor? What's more, it just so happens that my new connection is also a vice president in a large publishing company!

See, that's just another example of what can happen when we take the time to listen and then connect what we learn with what we know for the benefit of someone else. Is there a magic bullet to this connection process? Some sort of secret formula that makes contacts, sales, and profits magically materialize? Sorry, no. Work is still work, and it takes a lot of effort.

Learning to check our ego at the door so we can listen more and talk less is a good start. But keeping track of thousands of relationships simply requires a lot of work and constant organization and follow-up. Forget to connect and the relationship disappears. Write an important name and telephone number on a bar napkin and your next great idea may end up in the trash with the used swizzle sticks!

Many of the ideas in the chapters of this book won't necessarily make your day easier, but they will make the work you do more effective and profitable. *Building Relationships That Last a Lifetime* is about connecting with people farther and deeper than many of you ever considered. Taking a real interest in the other guy and making a deliberate effort to build a relationship with that person will change your life and every life you touch.

Your next connection could change the entire world. It's up to you to take the first step.

My name is Ron Rice, and this is my story.

1

Knowing the Difference between a Good Riding Lawn Mower and a Great Computer System

First off, let me tell you that I am a man who is living the American dream. My parents did too, but we did so using different methods. All I can say is that only in America could a man with my background, family contacts, and education earn millions of dollars in a technology that I knew very little about.

Both of my parents were hardworking children of coal miner families from Pennsylvania. As they grew older, they found themselves with little education and even fewer employment options. My parents had two roads they could follow: the coal mines of western Pennsylvania or the auto plants of Detroit. My grandfather had determined early on that his two sons would not follow previous generations into the coal mines, so my dad and his older brother struck off for the promised land of factory jobs and good money building cars of the mid-1950s in the motor city.

The car companies provided my family a good life. Both of my parents worked in the auto industry, my dad at Cadillac and my mother at Ford.

Earning two paychecks allowed us to live in a nice home, send my sister and me to Christian schools, and even take piano lessons. I'll never forget my father's two life dreams when he left the farm: indoor hot water and a swimming pool in the backyard. Thanks to the auto boom of the 1960s and '70s, he achieved both.

Having two hardworking, strong Christian parents gave me some decided advantages in life. No question about it. We always had everything a kid ever needed, and my education was top-notch. I never really struggled in school, but I did suffer from a lack of direction in my young life. Despite my decent grades, it appeared that I too would follow my parents into the auto plants and join the thousands on the assembly line. Until one day during my junior year in high school when I decided to take a summer job in the sales business. Not many high school kids can say this, but I can honestly say that this particular summer job changed the direction of my future life's work.

Summer Job

During this summer, a neighbor offered me a part-time position selling Kirby vacuum cleaners door to door. Figuring that this would be better than flipping burgers or mowing lawns, I decided to take him up on the offer. Thankfully, I was training with a master relationship builder. Rich was one of Kirby's top salesmen, and he cleared a six-figure income without much difficulty.

Rich showed me the trade by real-life examples. I followed him everywhere he went. I memorized his every word and action and made them my own in a very short span of time. My training was intense, short, and brutally honest. "Sink or swim" was our office battle cry. I learned to swim.

Since selling vacuums was a commission-only business proposition, starvation was also a great motivator in my early professional career. No sales, no paycheck! But despite being a tough trainer, Rich was interested in seeing me progress as a young man and as a salesperson. He may not have realized it at the time, but he was laying the foundations that would benefit hundreds of future professionals around the world based on his excellent example. I still use some of his phrases today when I talk to relationship builders of the future.

Although I was terrified at first, I started making sales to people other than family members rather quickly, and after a few tries and some refining of my sales presentation, I took to the business like a duck to water. I also learned how to run with a twenty-pound vacuum cleaner and accessory bag as an added bonus to my new sales career. Big dogs never seemed to care much for door-to-door salespeople, and I dodged a few in those early days and stayed in good shape hauling my wares.

After selling twenty-one machines in my third full month, I even won a trip to Jamaica! At seventeen, my parents vetoed the trip, so the boss gave me the cash equivalent and took the trip himself.

Earning over three thousand dollars in one month was a tremendous confidence builder for me, and it looked like going to college was not going to be part of my future. Generally, salesmen were thought of as people to be avoided in my family. Ron and Sally Rice's son was going to be a doctor, lawyer, or an engineer, not a door-to-door salesman. There had never been a college graduate in my family, and my parents were determined that I was going to be the first regardless of my sales success.

My dad was a soft-spoken man who said little, but meant everything he said. When I did my first demonstration for him of the wonderful Kirby vacuum in our living room, he sat quietly and shook his head. "Son, there is no way on God's green earth that someone is going to pay $550 for a vacuum cleaner!" I was disappointed, but I knew he would eventually come around. And he did, thanks to my mother. Incidentally, he had and used that Kirby for twenty years. Good products are still good products regardless of cost even when your sale is to your parents.

My father used to tell people that his boy was blessed with the gift of gab. "That kid can talk your ear off, and then start on the other side." "Oh, you'd better check your wallet after talking with this guy . . . That kid could sell ice to an Eskimo."

Over the next two years, I continued selling as I prepared to enter college. I had convinced myself that a college-educated doctor trumped a vacuum cleaner salesman. Since school was never a tough time for me, I decided to coast my way to a college degree and have a good time along the way.

College Days

My SAT scores were high enough to land me at Kalamazoo College enrolled in the pre-med program. Little did I know that becoming a doctor required dedication to the books and a lot of hard work. Remember how I took to vacuum cleaner sales like a duck to water? Picture the exact opposite, and that describes me in the pre-med program at one of the toughest schools in the country.

The only thing that went right at Kalamazoo was my relationship building. Everyone I met became a fast friend. I loved hanging out in the dorm, playing tennis as a long-shot fourth stringer on a nationally ranked team, or attending various social events. I was so busy with my social life that studying was a distant distraction. My grades quickly followed my lack of effort, and I received my first F on a Calculus test. I had never received an F on anything, and I was devastated.

Relationships could not replace study, and I knew my days were numbered. Fortunately, I was spending more and more time working at the college radio station and channeling my efforts into becoming a broadcaster. Finally I realized that college study was not for me. I contacted my dad in the middle of the night to announce my change in plans. My mother was in the hospital at the time, and we both agreed that now was not the time to tell her about my exodus from higher education. When I broke the news to her, she was supportive, but I knew I had let her down. There would not be an MD in her family this generation.

College lasted just two months, and though I did return and complete one full semester at Wheaton College, I never completed a college degree. This is still one of my life regrets. I have a lot of respect for a college-educated person. It takes discipline and effort to earn that sheepskin. Who knows, maybe someday I'll go back and get mine.

Radio DJ and Ad Salesman

I went straight from college to trade school and the wonderful world of radio. It took me nine months to get my FCC radiotelephone license and my first professional job in the Upper Peninsula of Michigan. I was on my way to radio stardom. I even had a radio name . . . Ron Nielsen!

As fate would have it, when I wasn't on the air the station manager offered me some extra cash to hit the streets and sell radio advertising. I could even sell spots on my own radio show and produce them myself. It was a great job and I loved every minute of it. I would pull my four-hour on-air shift, then grab a briefcase and hit the streets selling commercials. Since our entire staff was five people, everyone did everything at WGON.

Once again I was far more successful as a salesman than I ever was as a DJ. Relationship building was still a large part of my life even though no one really gave it much thought . . . even me!

I'll never forget my parents coming to visit and listening to my radio program as they arrived in town. My mother was very disappointed when I stopped by the hotel.

Building Relationships That Last A Lifetime

"I thought you said you were on the radio today?"
"Mom, I was on the air for the last four hours. Didn't you hear me?"
"No you were not," she said. *"There was some guy Ron Nielsen on the air!"* I started laughing. *"Mom . . . that was me! I'm Ron Nielsen!"*
After another twenty minutes of explaining why radio personalities sometimes change their name for fit and finish, we all had a good laugh. I still break out "Ron Nielsen" every now and then and flex my radio pipes. People still cannot believe it's really me behind the voice.

Radio was good to me, and I continued to hone my skills in building professional relationships.

Later that year, I married my high school sweetheart, Erin Simons. Even though she had just graduated high school, she decided to marry me and join a very interesting lifelong journey with a skinny blonde nineteen-year-old with a good radio voice and the gift of gab. I thank God every day for her decision.

The economy dealt a deathblow to the small radio station market in the early '80s, and it was time for me to find another line of work. Although I loved the radio business, the dollars just weren't there unless you could make the jump to the big city, and my skills just weren't that good. Erin helped supplement our income waiting tables or working in various office jobs, but I had to find a more reliable stream of income.

Mobile Wholesale Bicycle Sales Rep

One of my radio advertisers mentioned that his bicycle wholesaler was looking for a sales rep to cover the entire state of Michigan. I had an early love affair with the bicycle, so I decided to fly to Louisville, Kentucky, and interview for the job. Within two weeks, I was traveling the Great Lakes State selling bicycles, parts, and accessories to dealers across the state, building relationships as I went.

Leaving my young wife at home was not working, and we were both growing more and more unhappy with my new career. We missed each other during my long road trips. One holiday weekend, we were driving back to Detroit and our lives changed on the interstate. As we cruised south in holiday traffic, a large motor home came into view. We looked at each other, smiled . . . and knew this was the solution to our travel dilemma.

Our families thought we were a little nuts, but they supported our idea. When I called Louisville to run the idea by my boss, he loved it and wanted us to stop by headquarters as soon as possible to show off our new rig.

When we arrived in Louisville in our slightly used twenty-eight-foot Pace Arrow motor home, the owner was speechless. After a quick tour of our new home, the boss asked me to step into his office. The largest territory in the company had just become available, and since I was now completely mobile . . . it was mine! Instead of covering the state of Michigan, Erin and I were now responsible for every dealer west of the Mississippi.

Our travels spanned the entire central portion of the United States. From St. Paul in the north to Dallas in the south, we drove it all. When we would arrive in a larger city like St. Louis, we would set up camp at the local KOA, and I would load my briefcase on the back of my trusty Suzuki 370 motorcycle, and off into the city I would ride. After visiting the dealers in that particular area, we would pack up our rig and move on to the next town and start the process all over again. I know Erin would probably tell the story a little different, but it was an awesome chance to see the country, earn a good living, and be together every day. Our first child, Christine actually learned to walk in the store of a KOA campground in St. Louis. We still consider the owners of that campground "mom and dad" to this day some thirty years later.

Raising a child in a twenty-eight-foot motor home, however, did not seem like a good idea. Now that I think about it, it wasn't such a bad plan, but we decided to sell the rig and settle down somewhere in the Midwest and raise a family. Being from the Detroit area, we choose the suburbs of Chicago to make our home. It was close to family (three hundred miles) but far enough away for us to grow our own traditions and routines. We moved into a one-bedroom apartment across the street from Wheaton College.

I made my second attempt at higher education with a wife and young daughter watching my every move. With financial help from home, we survived our first semester, but it was tough taking a check from home and not working. So I decided to take the summer off and get a job to earn some cash and return to school in the fall.

I never returned to Wheaton College. The ad simply read: "Wanted: Individual with a good phone voice interested in learning computers."

Recruiter of Computer Programmers for Other Companies

I had a good telephone voice from my days in radio, and computers where an up and coming business. The PC was just starting to make small inroads into our vocabulary, and I knew computers would be a major force in the future, so I applied and got the job.

Building Relationships That Last A Lifetime

Technical recruiting (headhunting) was telephone sales at its best. My job was to locate computer programmers, talk to them about our clients, and explain why they offered a great place to work. If the candidate had the right technical qualifications, our job was to convince the candidates to interview, accept a job offer, and join the new company. For this service, our firm was paid a fee, and the successful recruiter a percentage thereof.

Recruiting offered unlimited earning potential, flexible hours, and the opportunity to work in the hottest industry on the planet with no end in sight—this was the place for me! The computer consulting industry continues to be loaded with talented computer engineers who have extensive education and training in complex systems. These talented individuals dwarf most of us when it comes to mental capacity and the ability to solve complex mathematical problems. It's amazing just how sharp these "nerds" really are. My success is due in large part to their tremendous knowledge and commitment to excellence.

I started recruiting computer programmers for various organizations in my early twenties. Even though I knew the buzzwords like COBOL, CICS, and IMS database, I would not know one of these technologies even if it mugged me in an alley. I was a relationship builder and not a technician. Although limited in my knowledge of what these technologists actually knew, I was very successful in finding, screening, and placing them with my clients. In less than two years, I had started my own recruiting firm and it was growing like wildfire with six full-time recruiters pounding the phones. Earning a million dollars a year was well within my reach.

Recruiter of Computer Programmers for Our New Company

And then one day, a former colleague of mine from the first recruiting firm we worked for walked into my small office with a business proposition. He was starting a technical consulting firm instead of a recruiting firm like the one we had both been trained in, and he wanted me to join him as head of sales and recruiting. This was a risky position since they had little experience and even fewer clients.

Instead of recruiting technical people to work for a client company and collecting a placement fee, my friend's new company hired the programmers to work for him. These technical wizards were not cheap, plus you had to have a generous benefit package to attract the best talent. In order to survive, you had to find clients with technical projects that needed an extra set of technical hands. The consultants got paid whether they were billing or not.

Bench time meant death time for a technical consulting company. Keep the gang billable at least forty hours a week and you might just make it.

The key was to hire the right technical people when the client's projects needed them. Then keep more clients and more projects coming so the consultants could finish one project and move to another with limited downtime. As the company grew, there was a constant start-and-stop project flow and a tremendous amount of coordination required to make it all work. Multiply that times five hundred consultants, and you can understand why there was never a dull day at Whittman-Hart.

My friend convinced me that building a technical consulting firm was a better way to go than building a technical recruiting company. The numbers sure looked good, and the new company was going to specialize in a special type of computer technology from IBM. The IBM System 38 (soon after the AS/400) was one of IBM's most successful business computer systems, and our new company specialized in this technology exclusively. As employee number thirteen (a lucky number) I became the firm's first full-time recruiter and salesman. My friend was one of three founding partners, and the only nontechnical boss. I left the recruiting company I was working for with my six-figure income to start a new position at $25,000 base pay plus commission and a promise of millions in the future.

My friend Bob Bernard and I shared an office, which was also the mailroom, copy center, and gathering place for any consultant passing through. Together, Bob and I found the clients, recruited and interviewed the consultants, and put the two sides together. I remember the large whiteboard we stared at as we dialed for dollars in those early days. Making the connections at the right time, right price, and right technology became a wildly successful part of my daily professional life.

What amazes everyone who ever met Bob and me was our lack of computer programming experience. Even the potential technical hires were amazed that their sales team knew very little about the technology we were working with. Here we were, two guys just old enough to buy a beer building one of the fastest growing technology firms in the country, and neither one of us could write one line of computer code, or even turn on an AS/400 computer!

By the time we were done, the company we started employed thousands of technical talent across every computer platform and technology. We had operations around the world, and in every major city in North America. Yet to this day, I could not tell you what a large computer system looks like, or really how it technically functions. I was never allowed in a computer room for fear of breaking something!

The Key to Success

The reason why I share this story is very important, and one of the main themes of this book: *Your ability to build relationships will determine your success or failure in life, not what you know.*

Bob Bernard and Ron Rice were blessed with the ability to sit down with anyone, anytime, and anywhere and start a working relationship. Some were wildly profitable and lasted many years, while others were very short and yielded little result.

Our seminar training from IBM, Xerox, and the Harvard Business School allowed us to communicate, listen, and detail in writing complex ideas and systems. We spent many hours working with clients to "smoke out" projects so our technical staff could design and build them. Some would say we were blessed with the gift of gab, but it was more than just a type A personality. It was systems, discipline, and an unwavering confidence in what we were doing, plus the ability to turn conversation into tangible projects that made the process work.

Since I knew nothing about the client's technology, I used this lack of skill to my advantage. I had to listen more and ask more questions than a seasoned technologist. We would start every client visit by stating categorically that I was not technical. Should the client wanted to talk deep technology, I would bring in two or three technical giants from our company and dazzle them with technical wizardry, or we could simply have a business conversation on how we could help the client get things done on time and on budget. We rarely took technical people on sales calls until we were ready to put together the technical project plan. It was never about the solution, cost, or method; it was always about the relationship and trust.

The same held true for our technical staff. They trusted us to do our jobs well so there would always be plenty of new work and new clients to keep them billable and technically challenged. We actually turned away certain business that was not tough enough to keep our technical team happy!

We *never* laid a single technical person off in my twenty years with the company. No matter how tight things were, letting someone go was never even discussed. It was my job, along with those who worked with me in sales, to get more business than we needed. If anyone was going to lose their job because of tough times, it was sales and never the consultants. These technical folks were our inventory, our bread and butter, and the backbone of the organization. It wasn't their fault if business was slow; it was the people in charge of building business relationships.

We were too young and stupid to ever realize that two uneducated phone jockeys could build one of the best organizations the technical world had ever seen, and convince hundreds of others to join us in a fantastic journey.

The Results of Applying Some Key Concepts Every Day

Bob Bernard adorned the cover of many business magazines. At one point, he was the fifth richest man under the age of forty in the United States, according to *Fortune* magazine.

I was fortunate to cash in my share of the company and retire at forty-two a multimillionaire. The computer consulting business was very good to the Rice family. Not knowing the difference between and good computer system and a riding lawn mower wasn't such a bad idea after all! Building many professional relationships over the years and helping them achieve their goals through computer technology made me a rich man.

Those who build relationships well and manage them like a science will achieve success beyond their wildest dreams. Those who do not understand the importance of doing this will not achieve their full potential no matter how well educated, experienced, or persistent they may be.

The following pages present certain relational concepts that will change your life if you simply apply these concepts in your daily routine. They were developed over twenty-five years of real-world experience. There is nothing difficult or mind-boggling in these techniques. What makes them work or fail is daily application and documentation. The process is so simple it's very easy to neglect the little things that make the entire process successful. "Knowledge without application is simply trivia" is one of my favorite quotes. Knowing something and applying something are two very different actions. Knowing is good for a board game, yet applying something changes the world.

The ability to develop and grow relationships will determine where you go in life both professionally and personally. Without other people, you will miss valuable experiences like teamwork, marriage, family, and church. All of these groups revolve around relationships. Relationships and their benefits are important to all of us. It is impossible to avoid them if we are still breathing. Most of us have many relationships. Some are strong and important, while others are nothing more than acquaintances, Regardless of the level or number, relationships are the most important human contacts we will ever experience. What we do with people we meet will determine the quality of our lives.

Reading This Book

The book is divided into twenty-three chapters grouped into three sections:

PART ONE talks about what relationships are, how they are developed, organized, and maintained (chapters 2–10).

PART TWO discusses building a business and the key relationships needed for the enterprise to succeed (chapters 11–15).

PART THREE, the final section, outlines seven skills that will change anyone willing to practice them on a regular basis (chapters 16–23).

Understanding the value and benefits of lifetime relationships will have a major impact on your life and the lives of those around you. Many ideas discussed in the following pages will be familiar and a few brand-new. Take time to bring them all together and apply them to your unique life situations.

Then pass it on!

PART ONE

Building Relationships
That Last a Lifetime

ෆ෪ඔ

2.

Why Relationship?

Humans are social creations. We were designed from the beginning to be in relationship with everything around us. All of us enjoy some quiet solitary time, but prolonged isolation makes us uncomfortable, and extended separation will eventually drive us insane.

Relationships Are a Lifelong Human Need

Studies have shown that newborns require human interaction shortly after birth for much more than food and protection. Provide nothing more than life support, and the child's personality and ability to learn and function will be damaged for life.

There are many examples of abandoned children who were kept isolated from the world and human contact for many years. When they were finally discovered by authorities, they were still infantile in their mannerisms, speech, and mental capacity. The actress Jodie Foster portrayed such a neglected individual from the backwoods of North Carolina in the film *Nell*. Even after years of intense therapy, Ms. Foster's character was never able to overcome her lack of relationship with the outside world.

The need for relationships lasts a lifetime. Many senior citizens placed in extended care facilities with little or no outside relationships quickly deteriorate in health and mental capacity, and go from vibrant, productive citizens to comatose vegetables. Volunteer organizations have sprung up all across the world to do nothing more than visit shut-ins, because the most basic human contact (relationship) makes a huge difference. No magic formula or training is required for success. Just a small amount of time on a regular basis that builds relationship improves the recipient's health and overall quality of life. Without this regular outside contact and relationship building, most humans will simply stop living. There are few of us who can last for any length of time, regardless of age, without regular human relationships. We all need people in our lives and the relationships they bring.

Relationships are not just for seniors; young people need them just as much to stay healthy. Youth mentoring organizations like Big Brothers Big Sisters exist simply to provide the basic relationship essentials to a child who needs them. Just being there makes the program work for thousands of children every day.

Relationships Are a Means of Influence

Relationships change lives. Many of us were dramatically changed by someone who took the time. Growing up, my best friend's father spent hours of quality time with us playing baseball, cooking pancakes, playing table tennis, and even coaching our League Little team. There was always time for a game of catch, tossing horseshoes, or watching a football game.

Mr. Lee Kenaga will always be one of my favorite men on this planet. Even today, in his mideighties, I still receive a good story or funny joke via e-mail from Mr. K. I cannot truly express my feelings for this dear man, and what he meant to me. His kindness and example set a high standard for what a father and man should be. I can never repay his wisdom, friendship, or leadership example in my life. His relationship with me formed a large part of the foundation of who I would become.

To understand the impact of relationships, we need to talk to those who have lived the longest and get their perspective. Most seniors' fondest memories and daily conversations are based on current or past relationships. They love to talk about their families, spouses, grandchildren, friends, war buddies, and other people who made an impact on their lives. Even if the individual mentioned in a conversation has passed away many years ago, their memory still burns bright in the mind of their old friend: "I remember him like it was yesterday."

If you look around the living space of a senior, there are usually tons of photos. The photographs fire cherished memories in the minds of their owners. "The good ole days" are recalled with each glance. The relationship may be fifty years old, but it still lives in the minds of those who helped build it.

You never hear a senior talk about money, houses, careers, or corporate conquests. Relationships that last a lifetime are the only things in life that really matter. Everything else will fade and pass away with time. Even death cannot erase an established relationship. The memories become legacies.

Relationships Make Memories That Become Legacies

My grandfather lived three hundred miles from my home. During summer recess, I spent time with my grandparents on their farm. I probably spent a grand total of fifty hours with my grandfather during my entire life, but those were good times. I have a coal miner statue in my study given to my mom by her father. My mother passed the statue to me, and it is the only thing I have of my grandfather's. Every time the coal black statue catches my eye, I remember "Pap."

My grandfather was a hardworking man who worked in a coal mine. He used to tell me about the cave-ins and how these were good events, since the coal was then easy to scoop up from the floor instead of having to dig it from the walls. Pap used to earn a penny a bucket, and the coal bucket was quite large. I cannot image how hard it was to feed seven children at a penny a bucket.

My grandparents lived on a small farm, so cows, chickens, and growing crops was a critical part of their survival, and an awesome place for a young city kid to visit in the summer. The first day on the farm would always start the same. Pap would take me to the local hardware store and buy me a shiny new Barlow pocket knife. "You can't be on the farm without a good knife," my grandfather would say. Being a city kid, we were never allowed to carry a pocket knife. It was a thrill to open the blade for the first time. Man, that sucker was sharp!

As soon as I returned to my home in the city, mom would pat me down and wisely take the pocket knife. God only knows the trouble I would have caused if she didn't. Fortunately, I've been able to purchase just about everything I ever wanted in life. My toy collection is pretty impressive: cars, racing boats, Harleys, lake and gulf coast homes, and luxury buses, but I still remember that silly little ten-dollar Barlow pocket knife like it was yesterday. I wish one of them would have slipped by the watchful eye of my mother.

Relationships have a way of doing that with our memories. Although I did not know Pap my grandfather very well, the time we did spend together must have been pretty special, because I still remember that gift and his presence in my life thirty years after his death. That was the legacy Curtis Emerich left me. He was my Pap.

What memories are your relationships building right now?

Relationships Can Even Transcend Death

Death has a way of exposing our memories of life's most important relationships. There was a large funeral for a friend of mine several years ago. The funeral parlor was jammed with hundreds of people sharing stories of this man, and doing their best to comfort his family. The man was in his midfifties and still had a lot of life to live. Unfortunately, he lost his battle with cancer.

During his funeral, there were no discussions about the houses he owned, the cars he drove, the millions he made, or the business empires he developed. All that was left was his family and the relationships he built during his lifetime. We never met in person, but his life was well spent. Clearly, building relationships was something he had taken seriously, and in turn, this made his life worth remembering. Who could doubt it? The room was packed with hundreds of people who knew him.

Story after story filled the funeral parlor like the sweet smell of turkey on Thanksgiving. It was intoxicating as people shared their favorite stories about their friend. Some were laughing, while others cried, but it all was a celebration of a life worth living—celebrated by the people who were touched by the man in the box.

Making a similar though more somber visit years later, I made a right when I should have made a left and ended up in the wrong viewing room of a large funeral parlor. Walking into the wrong room, I noticed a single vase of flowers, one visitor, and three signatures in the guest register. As I quickly made an exit, I noticed no one came to this man's viewing for two days! To punctuate this sad situation, as the funeral procession pulled away, the only vehicle that followed was a single minivan. Did this man have no friends, family, or co-workers? What happened? Did this poor fellow spend his whole life by himself? What a sad commentary on a life that appeared to end with no legacy or relationships.

Most of today's rich and powerful executives when interviewed will say that their greatest failure in life was not their business career; it was their relationships. Many have a string of broken marriages, children who do not speak to them, and a long line of personal relationships smashed to pieces on the altar of success. Perhaps as a coping mechanism, Hollywood has even made an art form out of the rich dysfunctional family. From the Osbornes to Hulk Hogan, the television screen presents a comical yet deeply sad depiction of life in the fast lane without real relationship.

One of the key measures of a life must include the relationships built and nurtured when a person was alive. Family, friends, business associates, teammates, and neighbors who were touched by us make up the legacy of our life. If we never cared or took time for others, did our life ever count for much of anything?

What if your funeral was tomorrow? How many people would validate the relationships you built during your lifetime? Would your last earthly shindig be a stadium event, or would a single minivan handle the crowd going to the cemetery?

Building relationships that last a lifetime is your legacy. What we do with our lives is important. Every life has tremendous value, and a strategic part to play.

The next chapter describes four types of relationships in life. Understanding how relationships are built as well as how to capture and improve them not only improves the quality of our own life, but also the lives of those around us. How well we seize each moment will determine our legacy, and the lasting impact on our world.

3.

The Four Types of Relationships

Dictionaries define the word *relationship* in terms of a connection, association, or involvement. They go further to mention an emotional or other type of connection between people.

Meaningful relationships cannot be group affairs. There are one-on-one journeys with give-and-take coming from both parties and both benefiting from the contact.

I have come to understand that there are four basic types of relationships to consider: spiritual, family, professional, and personal. All four types share many common traits, but each one has a uniqueness that distinguishes it from the others.

Spiritual Relationships:
The Mystery of Trusting Something You Cannot See

Spiritual relationships are relationships between people and God. If you do not believe in God, spiritual relationships are not part of your life, and that's a tragedy.

Set your alarm clock a little early tomorrow and take in a sunrise. No matter how scientific your view of the world has become, there is no way you can watch a sunrise and not believe in God. Events like that just don't happen by chance, and there are hundreds of them every day.

Take a quick peak in a telescope on a clear night. The order, majesty, and sheer size of the universe shout the existence of God. The fact that you can read this text, from the function of your eye to your brain to your ability to recall and communicate what you have read are all incredible designs from an all-powerful, all-knowing, and forever-present Creator.

Christians believe that God knows us like no other being in the universe. Our relationship is so special and unique that the Bible says that He knows us by name. Even the hairs of your head are numbered and well known by our heavenly Father.

The Bible also says that God sent His Son, Jesus Christ, to earth to pay our sin debt and the sin debt of the entire human race because He loved us and wanted an eternal relationship with His creation. Unfortunately, we humans have a sin problem that separates us from a perfect God. Although God made us perfect, He also gave us a choice of doing good or evil. Thanks to a little help from the Devil, Adam and Eve choose evil and death, and every human since then has been born with an inherited and terminal flaw. That flaw is sin. Left as we were, all mankind would die and be separated from our heavenly Father because of our sin. Thankfully, God loved us so much that He was willing to pay our debt with the painful death of His Son on a criminal's cross.

Every individual sees spiritual relationships a little differently. Even people of the same faith, denomination, creed, or sect see God from an individual vantage point. No matter what type of training or instruction we are given about spiritual relationships, our walk with God is unique.

In all spiritual relationships the idea of a "personal" relationship with God is the objective or goal. The more we seek, the more we find. There are, however, people who do not accept the fact that there is a God. These agnostics or atheists cannot accept God in any form, so for them, spiritual relationships are rejected at all levels.

Yet could someone who rejects the basic assumption that there is a God still have spiritual relationships? It would be interesting to ask some devout atheists how they feel when they see a sunrise over the Rocky Mountains, or what did they feel like the first time they saw the Grand Canyon? Was it all just an accident, or a big bang?

A spiritual relationship shouts from these magnificent creations. Some understand and seek more of this relationship, while others close their eyes and plug their ears to the voice of something far larger than themselves.

Building Relationships That Last A Lifetime

God himself loves relationships. He created the earth and all the things in it for the purpose of relationship. God loves to interact with His creation. The Bible says that God walked and talked with Adam in the cool of the day in the garden of Eden like they were good friends. Yet Adam and Eve chose poorly when they disobeyed God, and every human being since has been separated from our Father because of it. Sin makes having the perfect relationship impossible.

God cannot dwell when sin is present. It is against His entire nature. He hates sin and what it does to everything it contacts. God never hated us, just our sin, so naturally He sent His Son to pay the ultimate price for all of us so we can be reunited with Him in a perfect relationship that will last for all eternity.

For those who repent from sin and believe with faith toward God, the relationship is restored thanks to Jesus, and we will walk with God hand in hand again in heaven just like Adam and Eve did in the garden.

Many experts feel spiritual relationships are the foundation of all relationships. I would agree. When the development process of your spiritual relationship is functioning and growing, every other relationship type benefits as a result.

Family Relationships:
Blood Should Be Thicker Than Water

Our first family relationship starts at birth with our parents. If we are fortunate to have brothers, sisters, cousins, aunts, uncles, and grandparents, our family relationships can be quite numerous. Many will last our entire lives.

Family relationships share a common ancestry, name, and DNA history. Parents teach children what relationships are and how to build them. When we marry, two families become one extended group. Marriage brings another set of parents, brothers and sisters, and an entire clan of uncles, aunts, and cousins. Although the blood connection does not exist, the emotional bonds can be quite strong and lasting. Many in-law relationships are stronger than the birthright connections.

Family relationships must be developed just like any other form of relationship. Just because you are born into a family, does not mean you have a family relationship. Like all other forms of relationship, family relationships must be made and maintained. Can family relationships go wrong? They certainly can. Even blood cannot overcome neglect. Time must be invested by both sides of any relationship for the relationship to grow.

The foundation of any relationship must be built with time, shared experiences, and service. Simple come-and-go contact during the holidays is not enough and will fail when the tough times come. Blood is thicker than water, but it cannot replace time and shared experience.

Professional Relationships: *Have Your People Call My People*

This book spends a great deal of time discussing techniques for building professional relationships. Although these skills apply to all types of relationships, most people relate them to salespeople or other relationship-minded professionals. Most of us have more professional relationships than any other type. Our contacts can number in the hundreds. Turning them from contacts to valuable partners in business separates a mediocre career from that of a superstar.

We will meet many people for the first time in a business relationship setting. Based on our relationship development work, some of these relationships can go on to become best friends (personal) or even husbands or wives (family). A former business relationship of mine even invited me to learn more about Jesus Christ (spiritual). Building solid business relationships can create great wealth and provide a tremendous amount of professional satisfaction.

The secret to my personal success was strong business relationships at all levels. No one knew more about the client than me, and I never stopped learning more with each conversation. Building relationships with people involved in the deal was always the objective. Taking notes, asking questions, and bringing the entire deal together was a passion. The key ingredient was taking what the client was saying and turning that into a business proposal.

Too many times in the field of computer consulting, technical staff solved the problem in their head instead of listening and asking questions. Many of our top technical people did not win many deals because they were busy solving instead of listening and building relationships. Make no mistake, we had some super technical people working with us, and they did some amazing things with computers. It was a team effort. Solid relationship-building strength combined with their technical brilliance. We were tough to beat.

Professional relationships are the key to success in any work endeavor. Being able to pick up the phone and talk to an expert is a great relationship to have. Building them takes time and a plan. Even if you are one of the most intelligent people on earth but have been avoiding building professional relationships, your talent will never realize its full potential. Working with others is the key to multiplying your success and your knowledge. You cannot get there in a vacuum or by living on an island.

Too many business relationships are quickly lost because of agendas. You cannot start any relationship with your own agenda. We must seek the other person's needs and desires first. Putting our needs and time lines second to someone else's builds relationship and success.

If you are a professional salesperson, remember to leave your brochures, cards, and prepared presentations in your briefcase. The key to selling anything is your ability to understand what the client needs *first!* If you arrive at a meeting with an agenda other than listening and asking questions, you are fighting a losing battle. Clear your mind of all that knowledge and become the dumbest person in the room. Ask questions, take great notes, and build a relationship that will allow you to serve and sell your entire life instead of just once.

Personal Relationships: *You Can Never Have Too Many Friends*

Personal relationships are our friends, and can be the most rewarding. The reward comes from sharing happiness and sometimes sorrow with another person over an extended period of time. Personal relationships are often very deep, emotional experiences.

Unlike family or business relationships that are often chosen for us, personal relationships are the ones we choose for ourselves. Many things we do to build a personal relationship are unplanned with little structure. They just seem to happen. Think about your best friends. You did not wake up one morning and decide you needed one. They just appeared and the journey began.

We share common interest and enjoy the same things in our personal relationships. It could be a sports team, a hobby, shared interest with our children or spouses, or some other kind of enjoyable activity. Depending on your personality, you may have several good friends, or you may have only one. Some people make friends easily, while others are more laid back and develop friendships slowly.

Personal relationships are usually interesting reflections of our own personalities. Anyone who has ever met me would not consider me shy or laid back. My personality is as type A as you can get. I'm loud, gregarious, and really enjoy having a good time. I make sure everyone around me is doing the same. I love to speak in public, sing karaoke, and mingle with new people whenever and wherever possible.

Several of my close friends are just the opposite. Many of these guys are shy in a crowd. You'd never get them up on stage to sing karaoke or make a public speech without a lot of effort or a few cocktails. All of them love to see me make a fool out of myself while they watch from the crowd. Even as we were growing up, I always did most of the talking, and still do to this day. "Opposites attract" is a saying often used to describe this phenomenon.

All relationships, regardless of type, require work. The quality and depth of a relationship is directly proportional to the amount of effort both sides invest. Strong friendships, deep brother-sister bonds, and a closer walk with God Himself are all results of relationships that have time and effort invested. Strong relationships do not just happen. They require intentional effort and attention to the other's needs.

Life will present us opportunities for relationship in all four areas. These chance encounters are simply one-time contacts if we do not act. Contacts quickly fade from memory and die. It is up to us to grab hold and turn the chance contact into something more.

It's amazing how casual contact becomes a relationship and then changes again as we invest time and effort. A business relationship becomes personal. A personal relationship becomes family. Even a family relationship can turn into a business relationship, and back again.

The change occurs because of effort. Just like a farmer changing the barren ground into a productive field.

4.

Relationships and the Art of Farming

Building relationships that last a lifetime has a lot in common with farming.

Think about it. A farmer takes a piece of land and decides to grow corn. The raw land is littered with rocks, trees, stumps, and other debris. The ground may have other problems such as drainage or draught and need some type of irrigation. The land is not ready for anything close to growing crops. It needs work.

Farming: *Soil and Crop Cycles through the Seasons*

Whatever condition the land is in today, the farmer must prepare the ground before it becomes a field. Working with a tractor, horse, or even by hand, the farmer prepares the land, and with a lot of work, the land becomes a field that is ready for planting. Throwing seed on a piece of unprepared ground will not produce a good crop. You may get a few edible plants, but you will waste a lot of time and good seed.

Once the field is prepared, the farmer carefully lays out rows for the precious seeds using just the right amount of space for each row. Then each row is carefully sown to the right depth in the ground, and in a straight line. If the farmer were simply to scatter the seeds, future necessary steps—cultivation, fertilization, and the eventual harvest—would be difficult and less productive. Great care must be taken not to plant to shallow or too deep or else the seeds will never sprout. Even if the farmer completes every step to perfection, he still may lose the crop due to events beyond his control. God must provide the right amount of sun, rain, and temperature or the farmers work will be in vain.

After a few agonizing months, the corn or whatever was planted begins to sprout. The anticipation of food pushes the farmer to support the young shoots with cultivation, insecticide, and fertilizer.

Finally, the great day of harvest arrives, and the farmer reaps the results of his hard work. Many long days spent harvesting finally brings the crop into the barn. Most of what the farmer grows never reaches his table. Instead, it is shipped across the globe to feed people the farmer never knew.

Within weeks of the end of harvest, the farmer returns to his field to start the entire process once again. Farming is an ongoing sequence of events that stops only when the farmer or his customers are no longer hungry. Since we need food for our entire lives, the farmer's job is never really finished. It is a continuous circle of scheduled activities resulting in food.

Building Relationships: *People and Life Cycles through the Seasons*

Buildings relationships that last a lifetime is just like farming. Unless we plan on moving to a deserted island for the rest of our lives, relationship building is always a part of our daily lives.

When we go out into our world we have encounters with many different people on a daily basis. In the office, grocery store, school, church, parties, or simply walking the dog, we encounter thousands of people over our lifetimes. These encounters are the raw land the farmer surveys. Some contacts become fields and others remain barren ground. We choose what we will attempt to grow and what we will leave untouched. We decide on which it will be, whether a field or barren ground when it comes to relationships.

Once we meet someone whom we find interesting, unusual, or of potential value to us, we start the process of relationship building with a touch. A touch can be a simple "hello," or a question, "How are you today?" (We will talk more about touches in chapter 6.) If the new relationship continues to expand, we may spend some time learning about this new person and sharing some information about ourselves, our families, and our backgrounds, and in turn learning the same information from our new contact. The ground quickly becomes a field, and we are preparing the field for seed.

As our first meeting comes to an end, we decide that we would like to go on to the next step in building a relationship, and we schedule a follow-up meeting. This follow-up turns into a lunch, dinner, golf match, or taking the kids fishing. Whatever these steps are, we learn more and more about our new relationship with each encounter. We are planting the seeds of relationship.

As our relationship grows, we look for opportunities to help each other in life's pursuits, all the while connecting this relationship with others we have established over the years. We may even get our families involved: our spouse, kids, and brothers and sisters may all share in this relationship over the years. The young harvest is growing strong and tall, and starting to bear relationship results and projects.

Finally, something big happens. Together you and the person with whom you have developed your relationship do something important. It may be a business deal, it may be a charitable outreach, it may save a life, it may change one, but it is an important event to both parties. Harvest season has come to your relationship crop.

Maintaining Relationships: *Invitation to Continue Growing Together*

Like farming, once the harvest is completed, we start over again with the same relationship, looking for the next challenge you can conquer together. The relationship ground is now a productive field with a history of producing good crops. If we are diligent, it will be easier to work the field for many years, yielding good harvest that benefits many people in many different situations.

The relationship field must be worked on a regular basis to keep it healthy. Even a great field will quickly turn unproductive if neglected. Great things happen because someone decides to clear the land and plant a relationship. Not all contacts become relationships, however, and even well-intentioned relationships sometimes die. Some die from neglect, others simply were not meant to be. Since both sides of any relationship are human (except in spiritual relationships), anything can happen. Not all make it.

The farmer must continually repeat the steps to achieve a harvest in season. He cannot harvest only once, but must possess a discipline that understands the importance of the small, simple steps that yield success, and then plan for the future. Leave out a step, or count on someone else to do the work instead of yourself, and nothing grows.

Some of the best crops come from fields that started out less than perfect. Time is required for the true worth of a relationship to come out. A rocky start does not mean a rocky finish. The farmer continues this process as long as he wants to eat; so too the relationship farmer, as long as he wants lifelong relationships that add meaning to his life.

Farming and building relationships share many common traits. The farming analogy brings into focus the work required to keep relationships growing in our lives. It also illustrates the famine that can occur if we omit steps in the process or leave the business of others to others. We need to always remember: "It's not about us, it's about them."

If we really want to gain, we must give. If we really want to live, we must die to our selfishness. If we really want the bounty of strong relationships, then we must build them by seeking to serve and understand our fellow man, and we must do it first.

Here is how it's done.

5.

Straight Lines and Circles

There are two ways to develop relationships with people. One ends relationship quickly, and the other builds relationship for a lifetime. Let's examine both.

The Straight Line: *The Shortest Distance to Failure*

Building relationships that last a lifetime are never start-and-stop affairs. Unfortunately, we tend to make them this way and thereby lose the power of lasting relationship. I call this stop-and start-attempt the straight-line relationship method.

Hello ⟶ ~~Good-bye~~ "Till We Meet Again"

NEVER end any touch without scheduling the next one.
If you don't, the relationship will die. "Never say goodbye."

When we meet someone for the first time, we have the opportunity to quickly end the relationship or move forward in building it. If we decide that the individual is not someone we want to invest our time into, we can simply say "good-bye" and be on our way. We move from one dot (hello) across the line to the second and final dot (good-bye), and the relationship is dead. The problem with this method of engaging people is obvious. It stops and

33

in most cases never starts again. Unless chance allows us to bump into this person, the relationship is lost forever. In most cases, we wipe the person from our mind within seconds of our parting. We may encounter the same individual just days later and not even remember ever meeting the person. That's how quickly our minds shed untouched information.

Think of your own life and people you have met. How many times has a complete stranger come up to you and said, "Remember me?" We look at the person's face but have no clue where we met this person or what we talked about. Embarrassment quickly sets in as we look for a way to recoup. Hopefully, the contact will give us their name and the occasion of our last meeting, or just let us hang there and reap the harvest of our actions (or really the lack of taking action).

Straight lines kill relationships. We must be careful that those deaths are justified in our lives and the lives of our victims. Think about the server in the restaurant, or the flight attendant; how much time is invested in relationships with those who serve us? How many opportunities have we lost because we were in a hurry or too busy? Did we create casualties in those we brushed off?

Faulty First Impressions

Our hustle-bustle world has conditioned us to quickly evaluate people and accept or reject them within seconds. These snap judgments are usually wrong. Moreover, first impressions are usually wrong regardless if they were positive or negative. Only by spending time with someone can we actually assess what they are all about. Thirty seconds cannot tell the whole story. We need to listen more and talk less. The more we learn about the other guy, the more triggers our brain will have should we encounter them again. Our brains are fantastic data banks, but we must give them enough information input if we expect them to recall information when we need it.

For our part, we must be aware of the first impressions we create so we do not offend or drive off a potential relationship that offers great experiences for us. "You never get a second chance to make a first impression" is a very important rule for us all to keep in mind. We must be aware of our own bias and clear our muddy minds when we meet people for the first time. On the other hand, what we see must be clear and not rose-colored either. Fools see skin color, gender, or ethnic background before they see character and experience. Keeping our own shortcomings in check as we make relationship decisions is very important.

Building Relationships That Last A Lifetime

Bending Straight Lines into Circles

How do we avoid killing relationships in just one meeting? We take the straight line and bend it into a circle. We do this by offering our new contact a chance for another encounter with us. By offering a next step when we first meet someone, we give the other person a chance to enter into a future relationship with us. Since all meaningful relationships are two-way streets, both parties must have some level of interest to proceed. Offering a next step is as easy as adding a next step to the "good-bye" by offering an invitation to contact again. Here are a few examples of bending the line:

I enjoyed meeting you, let's get together again and talk some more.

I enjoyed meeting you. Do you have a business card?

I enjoyed meeting you. Here's my card, give me a call and we can talk further.

I enjoyed meeting you _____

You can fill in the blank with your own scenarios. The key step is the invitation to connect again. By offering a next step, you give the other person an opportunity to go further in building a relationship. The impression you make on a first contact can come full circle many years later.

A young programmer came in to interview for a job with our company. Although extremely bright, his technical ability was not enough for us to hire him. He was very impressed with our company, especially the written technical tests we gave every potential technical consultant. BALR Corporation was well known in Chicago for our technical strength. Our consultants were some of the top software engineers in the Chicago area. The reason our team was so good was because we made technical skills our top priority. From passing a series of technical tests to join us to an ongoing technical training program that was required for your entire career to large investments in hardware, software, books, and training materials, BALR was serious about technical acumen.

Even my two founding partners were born and bred software engineers, and they cloned themselves over one hundred times to make BALR Corporation a technical powerhouse. BALR's monthly company meetings always included a ritual unlike any other company I've ever seen. At the end of the meeting, one of the top technical guys would walk to a whiteboard and write out a line of computer code. Somewhere in the code was an error, and the challenge was not only to find it, but also to correct the flaw so the program would work.

As the old masters would sit in the back of the room with sneaky grins, the young technical turks would take a crack at the problem. Eventually, the problem would be solved and everyone (except me and the sales team) would learn something new. It was a great part of our meeting, and a great team-building exercise.

With all this cool technical stuff going on, it was easy to see why a young programmer would want to join our technical fun house, but this certain young man could not pass the technical exam. When I informed the candidate of his failure, he was disappointed. I reminded him that many people get tripped up on our exams, but he was welcome to come back in a few months and try again. He was happy to hear this and promised to come back. Although we tried to stay in touch with this fellow, he never returned to take a second swing at the C programming test.

Five years later, I was making my final pitch for a large piece of business at a division of a Fortune 500 company. We were in tough competition with a larger firm, and it looked bad for us to win the business. During our final meeting, that young programmer who failed the test walked into the room and sat down. I thought he looked familiar, but it had been over five years since his failed interview with our company, and I did not remember his name, or how I knew him.

As the meeting grew to a close, the mystery man rose to his feet and announced to the entire room that BALR Corporation was going to do this project. This former programmer was now a senior vice president and had hire/fire and budget responsibility for a department of seventy-five professionals and a budget of over $5 million! When quizzed by his own people how he knew we were technically better than other guys, he simply looked at me and smiled. I'll never forget his response.

"These guys are so good," the vice president proclaimed as he started laughing, "they wouldn't even hire me because my programming skills were so weak!" The whole room joined the VP in a good chuckle, but I could see we had gained a huge level of respect from his comments.

After the meeting ended, my new client walked over and asked if we could write some technical tests for his division, so they could hire "BALR-like" people for his team. I told him it would be our pleasure. As a footnote, he took the test again several weeks later and passed with flying colors. We spend the next five years doing many projects together as client and vendor.

That first contact with that young programmer was so positive that he remembered it for five years. Even though the first outcome was not a positive one, everyone had a big win in the end because a solid relationship of respect and professionalism was established in just one meeting.

Isn't that what we all are looking for . . . success in the long run? Many of your lifelong relationships will take many failures before they produce results.

Remember meeting your wife or husband for the first time? I remember chasing my future wife for our first date. She did not seem very interested in a relationship of any kind, but I did not give up with the first "no." I'm sure all of my married readers could share similar stories. Sometimes our first attempt at relationship is rejected. Don't be afraid to try again.

Evaluating and Dealing with Problem Relationships

However, there are certain relationships that must be avoided. But we must be careful to identify the problem relationships and distinguish them from the meaningful ones. To do this try asking yourself several simple questions: Why did I meet this person today? Was it fate, fortune, or coincidence? Was the meeting for my benefit, or the other persons?

When we evaluate the answers to these questions, we must be careful that we are not making selfish, self-serving decisions when we decide to cut off a relationship after one encounter, because relationships may have a bumpy start, and then later grow into something spectacular.

There is only one reason to cut someone off from all future relationship. That reason is illegal or unethical activity. Life is too short to waste time with crooks. If you happen upon such a bad relationship situation, you must take great care not to get caught up with this relationship no matter how appealing it may appear. Evil loves company, and so do relationships that are based on bad decisions. Drugs, booze, pornography, infidelity, gambling, or petty crime can suck the most well-meaning friend into quicksand. Hanging with a relationship trapped in one or more of these danger areas usually takes everyone involved down the toilet.

If you find yourself falling into a bad relationship, get help immediately. Talk to your pastor, trusted friends and associates, even professionals such as attorneys for assistance. Have them come with you to confront and remove this person from your life as soon as possible.

Also, when dealing with a problem relationship, think groups. There is strength in numbers, and the outcome has a much better chance of achieving a positive result when you intentionally involve other people to help you deal with troubled relationships.

Trying to rehabilitate people who are in legal or ethical trouble is serious business and requires experience and often professional training. Do not attempt this difficult task unless you are a trained professional, or at least without involving trained professionals to help. Working with others in a team approach is the only way most of us should ever continue an unhealthy relationship. Too many times, people remain in these dangerous scenarios and either adapt to bad behavior or become addicted to the self-destructive behavior themselves. Don't go it alone, either separate yourself, or get lots of help.

Do we straight line ourselves into a lonely cave, or are we willing to go to the next step and learn more about the new person standing in front of us. Do we say "good bye" or do we take the adventure of a new relationship and say "see you again." Let's choose wisely. A life-changing opportunity could be standing in front of us if we are willing to go a little farther. If your answer is "See you again," then it's time to bend that straight line into a circle.

The Relationship Circle

What you see in the illustration is a visual history and plan for one relationship. I call it a relationship circle. (This is not to be confused with Google Circles where you share different things with different people—a social-media attempt to simulate real-life relationships online.) A relationship circle illustrates the art of building relationships that last a lifetime. See how the arrows go around the circle. You will also notice that there is no end. Like the circle, a lifelong relationship has no end. Once we make the decision to allow someone into a relationship circle, it is our responsibility to make sure they never fall out.

The boxes represent a contact or touch, and they are critical pieces of the relationship formula. Studies show that we must touch an individual at least seven times before we begin to establish trust. Trust is the foundation of all lasting relationships.

A touch can be your first meeting with someone, a phone conversation, a letter, or an e-mail. We will cover touches in great detail in the next chapter, but for now let's consider a touch to be any activity between you and someone else that builds a relationship.

Building Relationships That Last A Lifetime

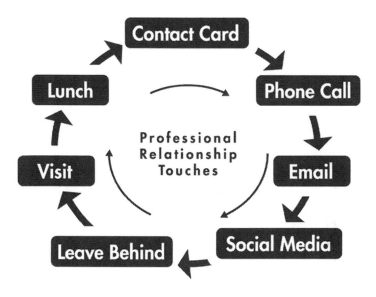

Now apply the basic model for a successful relationship to a business example.

As we discussed in the previous chapter, building relationships that last a lifetime requires an invitation to continue at the end of each contact. As you see in the diagram, we always schedule our next contact (touch) before we end our current contact. This follow-up is critical to avoid the straight line and thus death to any lasting relationship. Even if the next touch is next month, it is still scheduled and completed.

Write It Down or It Is Gone

Keeping track of these important touch times requires an organized system and personal devotion to the religion of writing things down. It is critical to take notes of things that are important in your life. Writing details, plans, numbers, goals, and to-do lists are some of the most powerful things an individual can do to change their life. By taking written notes, you turn intangible ideas into tangible documentation. Writing makes thoughts and ideas come to life.

Too many times people rely on their memory for important follow-up activities. This is sure folly. Our minds are wonderful creations, but they are fallible, and we *will* forget. By taking time to think and write about a single relationship step (touch), you are bringing together many different pieces of your background and experience and using them in an organized approach.

Desktop computers, laptops, and particularly PC tablets and PDAs (personal digital assistants) are increasingly used as electronic note-taking alternatives to good old-fashioned pen and paper. There are various types of note-taking software apps such as Evernote, Microsoft OneNote, Google Notebook, and Workflowy that we can use to help accomplish this task and organize personal info and notes as we build lasting relationships with people living and working in today's wired world.

What is so powerful about the relationship circle is its continuous nature. It never ends, so we need a written history of each circle to track our efforts and progress. Each time we work our way around the circle we add more and more touches, which build stronger and stronger relationships. If we graphed every touch on our circle for a long-lived relationship, we would have hundreds of touch boxes. Some would be the same activity like remembering our relationship's birthday, while other touch boxes would be special events like a golf match or baseball game shared together. Without a written history, circles return to straight lines and the relationship is in serious trouble.

Just like our farmer, we continue the touch cycle year after year and expect positive results. The farmer may even decide to change his crop one season. No problem; the process is the same. Relationships are no different. Relationships can also change with the same individual such as a business relationship becoming a personal one or vice versa.

One of the keys to building relationships that last a lifetime is learning more and more about the other person. We do this by asking questions and recording answers. By showing sincere interest in the lives of people with whom we have relationships, we understand what's important to them. Relationships are always about the other guy, and never about us. Every time we come in contact with our relationships we have the opportunity to learn more about them. We must take advantage of this and learn more.

If we manage many relationships at one time, like those in business, we must keep detailed accounts of every touch. If you are doing the data collection correctly, a business relationship will generate one page of notes or an equivalent amount of keyed information for every year the relationship is in development. All of this information should be in writing and organized for easy retrieval. These organized data sheets are called profiles.

We will discuss profiles in detail later in the book (see chapter 7). Needless to say profiles are vital to all business relationships and the building blocks for a successful career. Keeping profiles on our personal and family relationships can be a good idea also. Did you ever forget your mother's birthday? Your memory will fail you; however, an organized profile linked to a calendar will not. Yet this can be tricky to do well in our social media age. Facebook prompts users to wish so-and-so a happy birthday, but how then do you overcome giving the impression that the only reason you remembered is because Facebook reminded you? Something simple yet creative may be required in this environment.

When we look at the relationship circle, we must understand the fact that strong relationships take years to build. It's too bad that many people try to shortcut the process and lose not only respect, but reputation as well. These quick-hit closers I call the "thirty-second straight liners."

The Wrong Way: Thirty-Second Straight Liners

Trying to reach a level of trust in one meeting is ridiculous. Yet people attempt this slam-dunk approach every day. The quick-hit approach unsurprisingly looks like a straight line and usually ends with a "no" and at least one offended party. Even if the quick hit results in some form of a sale, date, or agreement, the lack of relationship will prohibit any future work together. Some people will say yes just to get rid of a strong-arm relationship. Many states allow a buyer to "change their mind" about a sale and void a valid sales contract within forty-eight hours. The law was necessary because companies trained their salespeople to take no prisoners.

This foolish way of conducting business continues to give professional salespeople a black eye. I do not blame the salespeople. I blame their trainers.

Why are most people offended by telemarketers? Simple. We feel uncomfortable being asked to do anything by strangers we do not know or trust. Every new relationship starts with two strangers. The two strangers become strong business partners, a married couple, or best friends based on time and shared experiences. If we accept these rules for relationships, a thirty-second phone conversation would never trigger us to do anything other than schedule another conversation to learn more, yet many of us still fall into the trap and end up disappointed and angry.

Telemarketers rely on numbers. People participate in the telemarketers offer for the wrong reasons. They buy to get rid of the relationship (the caller) instead of buying because of an established relationship armed with knowledge. Agreeing to an action to get rid of someone is always a bad idea. Here is why. By allowing yourself to be pressured, you allow bad behavior to succeed. This little victory for the one-sided user only emboldens them to keep it up with their next victim.

People actual develop a miserable career of slapping others into sales. I'm still amazed when I get an unsolicited telephone call from a stockbroker. Knowing virtually nothing about me as a person, investor, or businessman, such callers actually ask me to do business with them. I normally take a few minutes and try to appeal to the senseless nature of their call and approach, but most are tied to a well-rehearsed script that is designed to pressure, but usually only poisons any chance for relationship or business.

Movies have been made about people who use these boiler-room tactics. They are always portrayed as true scumbags with dishonest and even illegal objectives. This is not how all telephone salespeople operate, but it is becoming a disturbing trend. Things are so bad for some that laws have been passed allowing individuals to list their numbers on a national "don't call" database that makes a telephone solicitation illegal. All because a few misguided organizations think that a thirty-second telephone call is the right way to sell products or services. We shall see it is not.

If a company wishes to use the telephone to secure new clients, the first call must be an introduction and fact-finding call, period. No solicitations. If the prospect is interested after the initial call, then the telemarketer should schedule a follow-up conversation with a specific agenda. The same circle of touches applies to the telemarketer as to face-to-face salespeople. The slam-bam technique works only once!

Don't allow telephone hucksters into your life. If you are one of these one-shot wonders, read on—there is a far more profitable and rewarding way to do business. So let's focus on building relationships, and not destroying them.

The Right Way: Time + Effort + Touches = Relationship of Earned Trust

Since I singled out the brokerage industry telesales people, let me tell a winning relationship story about a young broker who did it the right way.

Chris was a young college graduate starting his own office with a large national investment firm. Despite the firm's solid reputation, each new broker had to build his own book of clients by cold calling and street canvassing (door-to-door).

I was enjoying a beautiful summer day doing one of my favorite household chores, mowing the grass. I was just finishing up a nicely done crosscut when a young guy in a dark suit and tie (it was over 90°F) walked up and introduced himself. After his corny, canned introduction and invitation to "review" my investment portfolio and retirement strategy, I began to undress this door-to-door huckster with every sales and relationship platitude I could think of. (I can recite about a hundred.)

This young guy was going door-to-door on a blistering hot summer day getting his card and information out to build his new business. His approach was fine right up to the point where he attempted to do business. Since this was his first contact, he had a snowball's chance in 95° heat to close any business without trust. He could not develop trust until he earned it.

Just like a starving farmer, Chris needed to clear the land, plant some seed, pray for rain and sunshine, and then and only then could he eat, or in Chris's case, ask for my investment business.

Since the kid was standing there sincerely sweating, I asked him if he was really serious about earning my business. He finally gave me the answer I was looking for: "What does it take to earn your business, Mr. Rice?"

Well he asked for it, so Chris spent that entire afternoon on my front porch listening to an old sales zealot share much of the material in this book.

Over the next three years, Chris religiously reached out and touched me every ninety days. As we talked, I learned more about him, his company, his investment style, and his plan for my money. He also learned about me, my wife, family, and retirement plans. Chris always contacted me on my birthday (a great time to connect with anyone).

After forty months of touches and continuous scheduled contacts, I gave Chris a small portion of my cash to manage. He was sincere, well organized, and he earned my trust. The rest is a real success story.

Today, Chris not only handles my entire IRA, but I've referred many people to his care. At thirty years of age, Chris is well on his way to being one of the top representatives of his firm, and a multimillionaire to boot!

Why will Chris be successful at whatever he pursues in life? He will succeed because he understands what it takes to build relationships that last a lifetime. Combine that with a servant's heart, and you have an unbeatable combination. His relationship base grows larger and larger with every contact. If he continues the discipline of the relationship circle, his potential is unlimited. I'm very proud of what he has accomplished, and even more excited about what he will do in the future.

As a young business owner, I remember trying to earn some first-time business from a large company. I made up my mind that I would do some business with this organization if it took me ten years to do so.

I organized my relationship circles into a plan, identified the individual decision makers, and went about developing a business relationship with them. This particular company had over fifty decision makers in one building! You can image what fifty interlocking circles looked like. My time estimate of ten years was a little off, because it took only five before they gave me a shot at a small project. Once we earned our stripes, we became a regular vendor for this large company.

There were over five hundred touches (phone calls, letters, proposals, lunches, visits, special mailings) involved to get that first project. Over the next ten years, we did over $20 million worth of business with this Fortune 500 company, and it was worth the five years of "not yets" to get it.

When we take our relationship development to a higher level, the relationship circle becomes very important. By organizing our efforts, we can guarantee that our investment in people is planned, executed, and has the highest probability of success even if it takes five years.

The best things in life always take time and extended effort. Beware of quick success when it comes to relationships. You are probably standing on thin ice.

Networking: *Linking Relationship Circles Together*

After you have established many ongoing relationship circles, you will have the opportunity to bring two of your relationships together. The popular term for this is *networking*. When you introduce two of your relationships, you are actually creating an entirely new one. This networked combination can be more powerful and profitable than the two individual relationships.

Why network relationships? The benefit of bringing two relationships together is best explained in an old saying: "Two heads are better than one." Bringing two relationships together allows both to benefit from the knowledge, experience, and insight of the other. Add your input to this new duo, and you have a powerful team of three. Then bring multiple relationships together to form teams, committees, and work groups, multiplies the network factor even more. Most often you will see multilevel networking in the business arena, but it can apply in any type of relationship. Managing networks of relationships will require more detailed circle and touch campaigns, but the end result is usually worth the effort.

There are some danger zones to watch for when you bring people together. One of the most common is human nature. While it may have been different once prior to the fall of humankind into sin, people are not trusting by design and are suspicious of new people and ideas. Most of us are a little defensive when we first meet someone and tend to clam up and guard ourselves. As a facilitator of a new network relationship, it's up to you to get both parties sharing information. With each conversation, relationship and mutual trust will begin to grow.

Another danger zone area to watch for is politics. People can be political when they are introduced into a network relationship. For whatever reason, they have an opinion that must be defended at all cost. Once again, the facilitator needs to keep the communication flowing and work through any differences in opinion while looking for common ground and compromise.

If you build relationships with large organizations, you will be networking contacts and relationships constantly. Different divisions, chains of command, and various project teams will all require bringing multiple relationships together to accomplish different objectives. Your skills as a relationship builder and organizer will be tested often, so you must be on your game. Mistakes are amplified when you have multiple relationships involved. Lose one, and you may lose them all.

If you are an experienced relationship builder, your contact database is large. This database can be of great use to others. When you are spending time with someone and asking them questions, make sure your questions are broad enough to understand how to serve the other guy.

My business was computer consulting, but I've helped my clients buy office furniture, copiers, real estate, legal services, and even season tickets to a sports team all by asking broad questions or making an offer to help such as:

What are your biggest challenges in the next ninety days?
It looks like we have everything covered in my area. What other areas in your company need help?
I have a huge contact base in the Chicago area, are you

having trouble getting the right company for that project?
Let me make a few calls on that and see what I can do.

Over the years I've collected thousands of contacts from limo drivers to powerful political figures. By offering to serve others outside my profit zone, I strengthen my relationships through service. Is there any better use of your contacts?

When we look at relationships as circles, we understand the key to building relationships that last a lifetime. The key is continuous activity. We never complete the journey when it comes to building relationships. The circle has no end, just the next touch. The same continued activity could also be compared with service. When do we stop serving others? Most of us would agree that service, like relationship building, goes on our entire lives.

Once we have put away the start-stop way of treating people, wonderful things start to happen. The way we see people starts to change. The way we respond and react changes as well. When we put things in the context of a lifetime, little irritations and problems in others don't seem such a big deal anymore. It helps when we view relationships as marathons and not sprints.

Building relationships that mean something takes a planned effort with scheduled "touches" on a regular basis. Leaving our relationships to chance leaves us with few successes while we wait for the phone to ring. Our world is full of one-hit wonders and one-night stands. Why not plan our relationship development and organize our efforts? The results are worth it both today and tomorrow.

6.

Reach Out and Touch Someone

When I was getting started with my computer consulting business and making lots of phone calls (since that, snail mail, and door-to-door were all there was back then), the N. W. Ayer agency developed and ran an ad campaign for AT&T featuring the now famous slogan "Reach Out and Touch Someone." While the campaign strategy probably worked well to soften AT&T's image given its potential at the time to monopolize the telecommunications industry, one of the business goals was obviously to get more people to make long-distance telephone calls. This tagline expressed what media philosopher Marshall McLuhan believed to be true about audio and video communications, namely, that the telephone had "tactile power" and would extend touch (as in personal "contact").[1]

What Is a Touch?

We briefly introduced what a touch is in the previous chapter. A *touch* is a contact with someone else for the purpose of building relationship.

There are a variety of ways to touch someone to build relationship. They can vary from a simple form letter to a multimillion dollar grant. They can last less than a minute, or an entire week. It depends on the relationship, and the objective of the person providing the touch.

Every time we touch someone something happens. The happening can be positive or negative. There is no neutral. A positive touch builds strength in any relationship. Negative touches crack the foundation of the relationship. If we are serious about building relationships that last a lifetime, then we must know the difference.

Every time we touch a relationship, two critical events must happen for the touch to yield a positive result. First, we must learn more about the other person. Every touch should increase our knowledge database on our contact. Ask good questions, and take great notes with every touch. Learn more and more about the contact's past, family, hobbies, and their professional goals and ambitions. Most personal questions are not appropriate until many touches have occurred. Keep your inquiries light and open in the early phases of the relationship. Be open to share information about your background if asked, but remember it's about them and not about us.

The second critical event in every touch is scheduling the next one as part of the current touch. Never initiate a relationship touch without a plan to schedule the next encounter. Whether a telephone call, visit, or first date, always have the next step teed up before you complete the touch and ask permission to touch again in the future as part of your good-bye.

As I have mentioned, there are various kinds of touches. Here are a number of examples described and illustrated.

A Telephone Call Touch

The telephone is one of the greatest inventions ever created for developing relationships. Telephone calls are a great way to touch someone. You can gather information, give advice, and generally improve a situation with one phone call. A telephone call is also cost efficient. Driving cross-country to say "hello" can be very expensive. It also takes a lot of time. Telephone conversations are inexpensive and extremely time efficient.

Telephone calls cannot build strong relationships by themselves. Other types of touches must be used along with the telephone calls to be effective, but the telephone call is a great way to follow up and stay in touch.

There is a danger area when it comes to using the telephone. The danger is neglected planning, because dialing the phone is so easy we don't plan our conversations first. Before you dial that number, plan your call. What is the reason for the call? What questions have you prepared? What is your follow-up step to schedule before you complete the call? Even if the call lasts thirty seconds, there should always be a plan, objective, and follow-up strategy.

Building Relationships That Last A Lifetime

A few minutes of planning will make the telephone call touch powerful and build the relationship. Just winging it could cause relationships problems down the line.

If your job is building relationships for a profession, you must be an expert with the telephone to be successful. No call is ever made without a purpose, objective, and long-range plan, and no call is ever completed without scheduling that next touch.

The Letter

Sending a letter is a powerful touch. Always make sure you personally sign them to double your impact by showing personal attention and not a simple form program.

Having made a few cold calls in my years in sales, using a follow-up "thank-you" letter was a great way to keep the relationship moving forward. Nothing fancy or profound is required. A simple "thank-you" and a confirmation of your next touch is all it takes. If possible, make the letter personal by writing it in your own handwriting. My penmanship skills are pretty poor, so my letters were always typed, but personally signed. The more care your written touches appear, the more powerful they become.

It's a great idea to keep a collection of good letters you've received over the years on file and make them your own. Be careful not to sound like a form letter in your correspondence. Our goal is building relationships, and there is nothing "form" about any touch we use.

If you do not write well, your personal and professional career will be limited, so try to force yourself to write more. Practice makes perfect, and good writers are worth their weight in gold. Many local colleges offer business writing classes, so there is no excuse not to improve in this important area. Make the investment in your writing.

Building three companies from ground zero in my professional career required a crash course in business writing. "Crash" was a good word. Since I was one of the first employees in all three, I never had a personal secretary to write or type for me. Typing on a computer was a big deal. I had virtually no skills working with a keyboard or word processing software, so getting written projects completed was a huge time consumer. I worked hard to become a decent writer and typist. It took a few years, and a lot of mistakes, but developing that skill became a great asset throughout my personal and professional life.

Write your own material whenever possible. Something about writing it yourself activates sections of the brain for creativity and productivity. Learning to type fifty words a minute will take time, but anyone can do it, and it's a skill worth learning.

Today's students learn keyboard skills from early grade school, so by the time they reach college they can type with the best secretary. For those of us who went to school when typewriters were the norm, we will just have to work at it a little harder.

Writing is important when taking notes and writing in your journal (see chapter 11). Taking good notes, including writing down ideas and important information, is a critical skill in business, but few do it well. Once again, it's a matter of practice, practice, practice. Take time to write. The benefits are incredible, and using the written word as a touch is powerful.

The E-Mail Touch

The Internet has birthed an entire new industry of information. E-mail is just one of the thousands of benefits that networked computers bring.

If you use e-mail for a relationship touch, be careful not to use it too often. E-mails can be very sterile and cold. Computers can be programmed to generate e-mails themselves. This technique taken to the millions is known as spamming and is more annoying than junk mail. Avoid the temptation to use too much technology when it comes to a relationship touch.

Your e-mail touch should not replace a personal call, visit, or written letter. Use as many different touches as possible. Always include your complete contact information in every e-mail so people can respond easily. Setting up an e-mail signature that is automatically included with all new messages and replies is a helpful time-saver, plus this salutation also serves as an electronic or virtual business card, so make sure you use it.

The Card Touch

Whether you are the president of the United States, or the little old lady from Pasadena, everyone loves a good card. No matter what the occasion—birthday, promotion, sympathy, or just a plain old funny one—everyone loves to get a greeting card.

Standard thank-you cards can be shared by an entire office and are very inexpensive ways to communicate with others. A simple handwritten note inside the card recognizes someone for spending time with you, making a referral, or simply doing something a little extra. By saying "thank you" in writing, you show respect and professionalism.

Remember what we are going for here. We want to make an impact on someone else's life. If we are serious about building relationships for a lifetime, then our touches need to be thought out and implemented with purpose. A special purpose card is always a great touch.

The Contact Card / Business Card Touch

Every adult should carry a contact card. If you work for a company, the contact card is your business card.

We gave my card to our children when we traveled. In case we ever got separated, my children knew to give this to a policeman, and they could always find their father.

There is no better way to encourage future contacts than giving a card with your contact information. When you carry them and give them away, you present a professional image interested in building future relationships. A person with a contact card commands respect and attention. Whether you are the CEO of a Fortune 500 or a small town store cashier, you should carry your own contact card.

If your company does not provide them, get your own. If you do not work for a company, get your own. A great relationship is just around the corner, and that fifty-dollar investment could change your life.

Scrambling for a piece of paper, a napkin, or matchbook to write down your telephone number is bush league. This type of data exchange gets lost, thrown in the trash, and quickly forgotten. It screams for a straight-line relationship that will be over in the next thirty seconds!

Contact cards are a *must-have* item to anyone who is interested in building a relationship that lasts a lifetime. Even if you never build a single business relationship, you still need a contact card. Remember, along with professional relationships there are three other types of relationships to build (spiritual, family, and personal), and all three will be developed better with your contact card.

The Visit Touch

One of the best ways to build a relationship with anyone is by spending time with them in person. Although arranging these touches can take some work, they are vital in building lifelong relationships. Spending time with people whom we have relationships with allows us the opportunity to share moments and experiences. Things like body language, eye contact, and a handshake all build relationship bonds that form strength.

Wasted time is one of the pitfalls with the visit touch. Poor planning and organization can make a visit not only a waste of time for you, but your relationships as well. I've never met anyone who has more than twenty-four hours in one day. That's all we get, and we need to use them wisely. If you schedule a visit touch, make sure you've planned for what needs to happen so both sides receive a benefit from the meeting.

In the computer consulting business, visiting our most active and productive clients made the most sense once every quarter. Computer projects seemed to run in three varieties of time: major projects (six to eighteen months), large projects (three to six months), and hot projects (two to eight weeks). However, visiting your clients more often is fine based on the need of the relationship, but always have a purpose for taking both parties' time.

Selling technical consulting services made sitting down with a client and talking about future needs and plans a great idea. By understanding the client's upcoming project needs, we could plan our need of manpower into the future. This process was never an exact science, but it sure beat the last-minute telephone call from a desperate customer begging for help when all of our manpower was already assigned somewhere else! When the client needed help, it was our job to have the right people with the right skills available at the right time. If we were sold out (a good thing for us), then the client had no choice but to call in our competition (a bad thing for us).

When planning your visits, try to group a couple of visits in one trip. Look at the map and try to schedule visits in geographic areas. This will cut your cost and time in half. Now when visiting, make sure you take time to take a walk around even if the visit is a personal or family relationship. "Taking the tour" can be very important in building a strong relationship. Everyone has something special in their home or office, and most of us like to show it off. It could be a car, boat, a special machine, a new addition, or some other special show-and-tell. Make sure to ask and take the time and have interest to see it. For business relationships, make a note in the client profile of that special item or feature. It could be a deal maker or breaker.

Our company had just opened our first office in Wisconsin, and we were making weekly trips from Chicago trying to land our first few accounts in this new territory. Although our company was well known and respected in the Windy City, we were the new kids on the block in the Cheese State.

My first sales visit to a large electric motor manufacturer is a perfect example of show-and-tell. The potential client I was going to see had the perfect computer system, right software packages, and competed in an industry we knew well, so we were a good fit for their business. When I made my first telephone call to request a meeting with the head of technology, he was not impressed with the work we had done in his industry, or his area of technology, but he agreed to give me thirty minutes the next week.

After driving three hundred miles from Chicago, I was hoping to make enough of an impression on my new northern prospect to get a crack at any future business he may have, but I knew being from the "big city" did not help my chances. As I entered the man's office, I noticed a rather large walleye hanging proudly behind his desk. Being originally from Michigan, I had tangled with a few of the "steely-eyed" devils myself, and felt comfortable talking about walleye fishing.

A quick note here: *Do not bulls— someone with whom you want a new relationship. If you're caught, your credibility goes out the window, possibly for good.*

After spending my allotted thirty minutes, asking questions and sharing briefly about our company and our plans to open an office in Wisconsin, the client was preparing to shake my hand and show me to the door. I politely thanked him for his time and assured him that I would follow up with him in the coming months.

As we turned to leave his office, I fired a show-and-tell: "That is one beautiful walleye, Mr. Jones. Did you catch her on live or artificial bait?"

It took about five seconds for this very quiet, soft-spoken executive to break out the largest grin I'd ever seen. "Caught her on a silver Mister Twister with a night crawler trailer," he then said. "It took me a good half an hour to land her."

We were friends for life!

Not only did my new fisherman client show me the additional pictures of his catch, he took me through the entire plant. I got to meet the head of manufacturing, distribution, purchasing, and to top the entire visit off, the president of the company! All thanks to meeting the client where they lived, and not where I assumed they did!

I tell that story all over the country, and it always gets a laugh or smile, but is their any better way to build relationships than sharing someone else's pride or passion? Know your fish, sports, current events, or industry news as much as possible. There is no better way to visit than sharing common knowledge or experiences.

Visits apply to all types of relationships. Our friends, family, and church all love to see us on a regular basis. Take time to plan and enjoy your visit. But remember, visits are just one type of touch. They neither replace nor eliminate the other touch steps in building credibility. A visit is just one touch. Yet it is the most powerful relationship builder of all the touches.

Document everything you discuss, learn, or see. This information will become priceless as the relationship grows. Don't forget to schedule your next action or touch with your client before you leave, and get it written down in both your calendars.

The Field Trip Touch

Remember school field trips as a kid? I loved field trips to places like the zoo, museums, and other interesting places with my classmates. Field trips make sense in terms of building relationships as well.

One of my greatest business relationship activities was time spent on the golf course with clients. These golf field trips not only gave us the opportunity to talk shop away from the distractions of the office, but they allowed me the chance to learn more about the person and not just the position.

I would invite groups of clients and my managers to join me for golf outings on a regular basis. I would pair my staff with select client personnel for an enjoyable round of golf. I was always careful to match personalities, golf ability, and temperament when assigning teams and competition. This was always about more than just golf. Other field trips included sporting events, seminars, and even a Christmas party or two.

Make sure you have established a good working relationship with anyone you invite on a field trip. Multiple people mean multiple personalities. Care must be taken when mixing them together to insure that there is a benefit and no harm. Since you are the host, it's your responsibility.

One of my favorite hobbies is traveling the country in my motor home. Ask anyone who knows me, and the motor home is usually mentioned somewhere in the conversation. One of my most popular field trips with clients and staff was the golf bus adventure. A partner of mine was a member of a beautiful golf course about a hundred miles from Chicago. I would invite four clients and four or my technical managers to spend the day playing golf. I would pick up the clients at their offices first thing in the morning in the motor home complete with fresh coffee and Danish pastry. After loading up the golf bags, I would drive my two foursomes through the rolling hills of northwest Illinois to the Galena territory and our destination.

Occasionally, our guests did not know each other, or the members of our staff, so the conversation was a little slow during the first few hours, but eventually things would start to warm up. Based on the group, we would select teams and arrange some golf matches, pairing people up in various ways to add a little competition to the day's activities. Rarely was business ever discussed on the way out.

We arrived at the golf course around 9:00 a.m. and teed off shortly thereafter. While we golfed, the motor home was cleared of the breakfast materials and set for the ride home with cold beverages and a huge sub sandwich or pizza for the ride home. We finished the round of golf by 2:00 p.m. and were back in the motor home and headed for home.

During the ride home the conversation was much more lively and full of laughter and tall tales from the day's activities. The beverages and food went down quickly, and the topic turned to the business of relationships. By the time we returned to the client's parking lots, projects were discussed, meetings set, and future action steps planned. All if this happened naturally and with very little push from me. I was amazed just how effective our little trip had become.

Over the years, we did this many times, and all with the same results. Even ten years later, we still get positive feedback from the BALR road trips to Galena. After we dropped off the clients, the entire BALR team would debrief in our own parking lot before we called it a day. Detailed notes were taken and exchanged, and follow-up plans were set in motion.

Do not wait till the next day after a field trip or any other touch. Even if the hour is late, take the time to collect your thoughts, data, and ideas as soon as the people with whom you are building relationship have left. Relying on memory, or someone else's notes, could cost you far more than the price of the outing in missed opportunities. Write it down!

Field trips are fantastic ways to touch, but they also take a large amount of time and planning to be effective. They deserve a look as part of your relationship building touch campaign.

RON RICE

The Giveaway Touch

I'm a huge fan of the giveaway. If you worked for me, you always had three things ready to giveaway.

1. Your business card
2. A company brochure (we had three sizes from pocket to life story)
3. A cool item with the company logo

The first two items are self-explanatory, but the third needs a little more explanation. The cool items were goodies that people would feel bad about if they threw them away. If you are in business, you need items like this for two reasons. First, giveaway goodies count as a touch. If you touch someone with a visit or telephone call, leaving or sending them a coffee mug counts as another touch. It's just another way of saying "Thank you for your time and the opportunity to build a future relationship."

Second, when they see the goody, they see you. Every time somebody you're building a relationship with uses your pen, coffee mug, golf balls, note pad, or whatever goody you choose, they see and think of you and your company. That's why you must think long and hard before using goodies. Great ones make you look good. Cheesy ones make you look, well, cheesy (that's bad).

Here is a quick list of giveaways that worked for me:

A book—Books are one of the best giveaways in the world. Make the subject of the book you choose something of interest to the receiver, not the giver.

A pen—My engineering partners argued over which one to choose for a week. I'm glad they did. Everyone loved my pens!

A shirt—Quality, quality, quality . . . make sure the shirt is the right size.

A sports item—Golf balls are the most popular sports giveaway item.

A desk doodad—Remember, desk doodads must be special enough not to end up in the trash.

A great test of a giveaway is retention. I knew we had a winning giveaway when I visited clients three months later and still saw my giveaway on their shelf or person. I loved it when clients would ask for more pens because they thought the BALR pen was the best they had ever used. When they used it, they thought of us. I gave them away by the box!

Building Relationships That Last A Lifetime

The Social Media Revolution

LinkedIn, Facebook, Twitter, and a host of new Internet-based "social media" sites have exploded into the world of relationship building. Those of us who are serious about building relationships of all types need to understand and effectively use this powerful new medium.

When these new technologies first hit the scene several years ago, I was not impressed. The "old school" caveman in me dismissed these new ways to "connect" as mere college chat groups with no place for the serious business professional . . . I was totally clueless.

Everyone in the professional world needs to be on LinkedIn, period.

Since joining this free online social network and using its services, I have reconnected with hundreds of former staff, clients, and old friends by simply "connecting" through this powerful system. As they say on their About Us webpage, "LinkedIn operates the world's largest professional network on the Internet with more than 150 million members in over 200 countries and territories." And it continues to grow every day. I'm truly amazed at just how powerful this service is.

Perhaps you found or purchased this book because of social media. In any case, take the time to learn and use these incredible social media sites. They offer huge opportunities to connect, and then touch your relationships on a regular basis.

Remember the Follow-Up

I cannot stress this enough or too often. When we touch someone in the relationship building process, we must remember to schedule the next touch *before* we complete the current activity.

When we send a card, the final thought should be about touching them again: "Bill, Happy Birthday! I hope you have a great day and many more to follow. I'll call you next week and get caught up."

Our touch should never be the last one unless we are attending their funeral! Always be thinking and doing ahead. If you are serious about building relationships, then you must be a zealot about scheduling your next touch. Don't forget to write your next touch down in a calendaring device, or you will forget.

When Is a Touch Not a Touch?

There are contacts we make that are not touches. These activities are centered on asking the relationship for something that benefits us. These activities are *not* touches and need to be approached very carefully.

When we ask for something, we test the strength of our relationship with another person. If the foundation of the relationship is strong with many touches, then we will not damage it by asking for action. However, if we ask before we have a strong relationship foundation, we will surely damage, or even end the relationship.

Here are a few examples of contacts made that are *not* a touch:

A close—This is a term used in sales. It means "close" the sale.

A referral—We ask a client or customer for names of others that benefit us.

A proposal—We send a written document explaining our services and price.

A favor—When we ask someone we have a personal relationship with to do something for us.

None of these activities are wrong. When we should use them depends on the work we have completed in building the relationship. If we have built trust first, then we can ask. If we have not built trust, then these areas should be avoided until we do.

More Stuff about the Telephone: *The Greatest Touch Ever Invented*

I wanted to hammer home a few more points about using the telephone because its use is so important. The telephone is a tremendous tool in developing relationships. We can touch hundreds of people without leaving the comfort of our office or home. Using the telephone to touch people requires a little practice. People get impressions from telephone calls from two sources: your voice and your message.

What does your voice sound like on the telephone? Is your pitch high or low? Do you speak fast or at a slower pace? Do you have an accent? Is your voice volume loud or soft? You can answer these questions by leaving yourself a voice mail message. Listen to yourself on the answering machine or voice messaging system. How does it sound? Anyone can make their telephone voice better with practice. I know leaving yourself voice mail to practice sounds a little strange, but it works. Also, make sure your greetings on your work phone and cell phone messaging systems are professional and pleasant to listen to.

People have commented about my voice many times. I make no apologies for the amount of time I spent practicing. It was very important in my business career, so I took the time to become the best telephone communicator I could. Members of my staff who were responsible for building relationships would constantly do mock telephone conversations with me playing the role of prospective client on the other line. I would be rude, quiet, fast, arrogant, shy, and mimic many other personality types so my people could practice their trade. The more practice time you put in, the more comfortable and professional you will become.

Voice Mail

If we are going to use the telephone in building relationships, then we will need to use voice mail as part of this plan. Many people feel uncomfortable leaving a voice mail message, but it is the best way to touch base with someone who is not there.

Just like mastering our telephone voice and technique, we need to practice leaving good voice mail messages. Practicing is simple: leave yourself voice mail and listen. The more we practice the better we become.

I always tried to leave an upbeat message when I heard the tone. Here are a few of my favorite voice mail messages. Notice I invite the other person to the next touch point:

Business Relationship

BEEP!

Hello Bob, this is Ron Rice . . . I hope things are going well with you and your team . . . It's time to get together and pick up our discussions about that payroll project. I've been pulling together some exciting ideas, and I'm looking forward to sharing them with you next week. I remember Tuesday mornings are good days for you . . . I'll plan on being in your office at 10:00. Have Karen [the assistant] give me a call and confirm, or drop me a quick call or e-mail when you get a second . . . See you Tuesday at 10:00 . . . Peace . . .

Family Relationship

BEEP!

Hello, Son. It's Dad. I just wanted to drop you a quick voice mail and tell you how much I love you and how proud I am of the young man you are becoming. Mother sends her love. Be safe, work hard, give us a call when you can. We love you.

Personal Relationship

BEEP!

Hey, buddy, it's Ron. Haven't heard from you in a while and wanted to give a call and catch up. Things are fine on this end. Give me a shout and let's catch lunch or chase the little ball. Miss you man . . . Talk with you soon.

You can develop your own voice mail style and make it your own. Use this important part of our daily lives to build relationship. If you have gone through the effort to dial the number, finish the task and leave a good message. Don't hang up when you hear the beep, it's show time!

Seven Touches to Build Trust

Now that we understand what a touch is and what a touch is not, it's time to make sure we understand why they are so important. Studies show that the average person must be "touched" at least seven times before they begin to trust the one who is touching them. That's right . . . seven times. That's three phone conversations, two visits, a letter, an e-mail—or some other combination of these or other touches.

Seven is the minimum. Many relationships will take many more touches to build trust. Remember that Fortune 500 company that took five hundred touches just to earn their trust to do our first project with them? The more people involved, the more touches it usually takes. Each relationship is unique and special based on the individual, setting, and depth of the relationship.

No one will ever establish a relationship with us if they do not trust us. If we try to push our point of view or ask our new contact to do something without building trust, we will most likely fail or damage any future opportunity to work with them. We must earn trust. It just doesn't happen. No matter what relationship we are building, trust must be earned. It never just happens, or lasts, without effort on both sides.

Trust is similar to true love; it doesn't just fall from the sky. There may be attraction, or even lust, but real love cannot happen without commitment. How many times have we been attracted to someone for a variety of wrong reasons? It may be their looks, accomplishments, or even their alma mater that attracts us to them in the beginning. However, after a few short minutes of conversation, we realize that this relationship is not what we were looking for, and we quickly end what we thought would be a "match" made in heaven.

Building Relationships That Last A Lifetime

Just like true love, trust takes time to develop. It just doesn't happen. If we want to have influence or change someone's mind, trust must be the key to our efforts. If we accept this as true, we must start building relationships with those we hope to influence. Without building relationships first, we can never truly change hearts, actions, or beliefs.

Every four years, America finds itself in the middle of a presidential campaign. The leading candidates typically bombard television, radio, the Internet, and every newspaper possible with their images, platforms, and promises. Candidates even leave voice mail messages in which they say they are calling "personally" to talk with you the voter. These are all touches!

Each candidate is also meeting with as many people as possible in person. Even a large stadium event counts as a touch although a very weak one. Do you recall whether you heard from the leading candidates at least seven times? I guarantee you have at least fifty touches before the election. Both candidates are trying to build trust from a distance. Only each individual voter will decide how effective they have been on Election Day.

Once we realize that relationships are made not found, we can begin to evaluate all of our relationships and make sure we are investing time and effort to make them stronger. Left alone, all relationships die. With organized effort, any relationship can be saved or made stronger. It is just a matter of effort and time.

Consider the following examples of building relationships through touch within each of the four types of relationships.

Spiritual

Many people go to church once a year, at Christmas. Why? Do we expect to have a relationship with God when we visit once a year on His Son's birthday?

One touch a year will not lead to a strong relationship with anyone . . . not even with God. In contrast, God says He is always "touching" us and wants a close relationship with everyone. Remember, true relationships are two-way exchanges.

One touch per year makes for a very weak and ineffective relationship.

Business

Hail the telemarketers! They cold call you at dinner and ask you to buy a magazine subscription, donate to a political cause, give toward the police or firefighter's foundation, contribute to the home for veterans, support your college alma mater, or help some other organization, and who knows what else.

How dare they ask me to do anything after just meeting me! There is no way I trust them, so why would I give them my credit card number?

Funny but sad that telemarketing companies, studies show, have no plans to "touch" you, build relationship, or do anything right in terms of relationships. They want to sell you once and quickly. They have no intention of ever talking with you again about the same product or service. Actually, most telemarketing firms sell your name and number to other telemarketers who can call you next week and insult your intelligence again!

Do yourself and the world a big favor. Get caller ID and never buy from these organizations. They do not deserve your business, because they are not interested in you, just your credit card number and their sales commission.

I need to clarify myself at this point about phone solicitations. There is a right way to do this if you don't have caller ID or happen to take one of these calls. If I receive a call from a salesperson asking me to do something, the only thing that telephone caller should ask me to do is allow a meeting and nothing more.

If I decide that the offer sounds interesting, then I will meet with the person at a scheduled time and give the caller a chance to earn my trust and future business. The meeting can be a teleconference meeting, but the salesperson had better be prepared to ask a lot of questions and get even more information before they cross that trust threshold and ask me to buy. I should have some information in my hand before their second telephone call so I too can be prepared with questions.

If the salesperson is willing to invest time in our new relationship to a level that earns my trust, then I have no problem receiving a cold call, and eventually purchasing a product or service over the phone. The meeting, however, must be set according to my schedule and not the salesperson's. This shows that the representative is willing to work for my trust and is willing to do the legwork to earn it.

There are very few telemarketing companies that are willing and able to do things the right way, so I have little use for them and rarely take their calls. I always hold out hope that some will grasp the whole concept of trust and relationship. It actually makes more revenue in the long run. Remember the circle?

Building Relationships That Last A Lifetime

Give me the thirty-second shove and you may sell me once. Build a relationship with me that lasts a lifetime and you can sell me a thousand times, and my family and friends as well. Which sounds better to you?

Personal

The 1960s changed the way men and women meet. Most reasonable thinking adults would agree that the changes were not positive. AIDS, divorce, single-parent homes, and rising suicide rates among our kids confirm that the way people are building personal relationships needs some serious work.

Today's society is filled with garbage when it comes to personal relationships. Too many young couples end up in the sack after barely being introduced. Sex has taken the place of real relationship and will be one of the key factors leading to the end of our American society, let alone Western civilization as we know it. Historically, the end of meaningful relationship building was also the beginning of the end for many other great civilizations, including the Egyptians, Greeks, Romans, Incas, and Aztecs.

Meaningful personal relationships take time, understanding, and service to ever make it more than a few months. Phone or cybersex, hook ups, and quickie divorces are the results of poor education and even worst, a breakdown of important values. As a society, we must stop trying to build relationships in thirty seconds. This is especially true in personal relationships. We need to check our selfishness and lust at the door, and instead spend quality time away from the bedroom if we want to build personal relationships that last a lifetime.

There is no shortcut to lifetime personal relationships. When we cut corners, we sidetrack real relationship for a fraud that ends up crushing everyone involved, including society as a whole.

If it lasts a lifetime, it takes more than a few hours to build.

Family

Why is Mother's Day so profitable for FTD? Simple. You can say "I love you, Mom" with a click of your computer mouse, and you don't even have to leave your office!

Seven touches is just the minimum to start building trust, and not the endgame. The quality of your family relationships is equal to the quality and quantity of your touches. Even our family relationships will not last if we take them for granted. Touching once or twice a year will not cut it. If we value these family relationships, we must make the investment to keep them healthy.

A song called "Cat's in the Cradle" by Harry Chapin tells about a dad who's gonna be home soon. His son learns to walk, throw a ball, and heads off to college always hoping his dad will be home soon. I play a pretty decent version of this '70s tune on the piano. I even sing the words not half bad for the unmusical ear.

When I play the song, it always brings a few tears to those who hear the lyrics. Those tears are memories of missed relationship opportunities with our parents, or our own children. We all have those less than perfect memories, and they all hurt.

Just because we are parents doesn't mean we have family relationships. Like all relationships, our family relationships need our time, attention, and the special touch that only a father or mother or son or daughter can bring.

When you comin' home dad?

Planning and Scheduling Your Touches = Campaign

If we bring touches and the relationship circle into one program of relationship development, we are looking at a campaign. Although campaigns are usually thought of in a business development scenario, they also fit well into personal, family, and even spiritual relationships. Let's focus on the business side first.

If we are interested in developing a business relationship with a company, a relationship campaign is the best way to get there. As we prepare our relationship circle, think about what type of touches make sense for the individual we are intent on developing a relationship with. All relationships circles start at the same place, the introduction.

When we meet a business potential for the first time, there are a few things we should always do. First, *let the other person talk more*. Too many times we talk too much. Why? Simple. We are our favorite subject! This type of behavior will not build relationship. In fact, the best way to turn off a first meeting is talking about / selling yourself first. People love to talk about themselves. We should let them.

If possible, take notes on what the other person is saying. By doing so, we are telling the person that we feel everything they say is important to us and we do not want to miss a thing. I have actually stopped someone in mid conversation to ask if it is okay to take a few notes. I have never been turned down or disappointed in the information I was able to gather.

When taking notes, it is best to use a paper and pen. Avoid using a recording device. I find that people feel uncomfortable when they are being recorded. Too many CIA or *Law and Order* television shows. Keep it simple and use the good old paper and pen.

If we have done our job during the introduction touch, we should come away with the some valuable information about our new relationship, and we are ready to schedule our next touch (contact) as we end our first conversation.

How do we set the agenda for the next touch? We use the information we just gathered. As you prepare to wrap up your first conversation, look at your notes and review what has been said, and draw some conclusions. Remember, we need to touch this person at least seven times before we get too heavy in any requests or suggestions, so our second touch should still stay light and open. Every touch should involve gathering more information about our relationship. So as we schedule a touch, it is always a good idea to establish some type of future agenda.

Here is an example: "Mr. Jones, I really enjoyed spending time with you today learning more about you, your department, and your company. I'd like to follow up with you in two weeks to talk more about that new building project you mentioned. Would Monday the 12th at 10:00 be a good time for me to call?"

This is a very simple statement with some powerful relationship-building meat. First, we thank Mr. Jones for his time. Time is valuable and he was gracious to share some with us. Second, we invite a follow-up that shows our interest and commitment. Third, we are exact with what comes next in the process. Always set future appointments as firm as possible. Don't be hazy, saying "I'll be in touch," "I'll talk to you in a couple of weeks," or "Let me get back to you." Don't use these statements. If you are fuzzy about what happens next, then your relationship will also be fuzzy. Be as precise as possible.

Now that the second touch is scheduled, and the agenda set, we can spend some time thinking about what the next touches need to look like. Always send a follow-up letter after every touch. Include your card and a giveaway that makes sense for the person receiving it. Congratulations! You completed your second touch without even talking to the person.

All business professionals should have a business card. Those cards should be with them wherever they are, twenty-four hours a day. You never know when opportunity knocks, so you need to be ready to make a great first impression. Nothing says "I respect you" more than offering your business card to a new contact. In Japan, not offering a business card is a sign of disrespect. I think it should be the same the world over.

I had a client who saved every business card I ever gave him. Since I always sent two business cards with every touch, he ended up with over one hundred cards in a five-year period. He kept them in his desk stacked up and held with a rubber band. He would pull the stack out now and then and give me a smile. I would always tease him about hoarding my cards instead of giving them to potential business referrals. He would always retort with a comment about these being his collection, and not for distribution.

If you are in the business of building relationships that last a lifetime, and we all should be in this business, then you need to go through boxes of business cards. How many seeds do you think a farmer plants? Your business cards are seeds.

In developing touch campaigns for large numbers of relationships, we do not have to perform each touch personally. Using computer databases, college interns, or well-organized assistants, a professional relationship builder can touch thousands of people. The key to large numbers of relationship circles is organization. We will talk more about organization skills and techniques later in this book, but for now let's just say that allowing someone else to do the work requires a well-planned system.

The only taboo in having others participate in touches is direct contact. Never have assistants, interns, or other staff members make your telephone calls or have direct contact with your relationships. When you do this you are saying that your time is too valuable to continue building this relationship, so I've delegated this to my assistant. You might as well just call the person and end all future contact on the spot.

If you have too many professional relationships to cover adequately, it may be time to bring on a partner, or hire another professional to join the team. It makes no sense to have thousands of contacts that are poorly covered. Either hire and train more relationship developers, or cut back the relationships. Both are viable strategies that are better than neglecting and offending people.

Allowing others to assist you in relationship campaigns is a great idea. Having your team handle the relationship itself is a bad idea. Organize your time, plan your day, and execute your tasks like a well-oiled machine. Have your team do data entry, send follow-up letters as well as birthday or greeting cards (always sign them all yourself), and set up your call and visit schedules. Relationships are built with one-on-one personal contact. Teams don't build relationships, individuals do.

The touch campaign in view here is so simple it often fails. The reason failure is so common is memory. We forget to schedule or follow through with the next touch because we rely on our brains instead of our written records. Once we forget the follow-up and the reason for it, the relationship is lost and goes back to square one.

The more success you experience, the more tempted you will be to stop writing and try to remember. This is a fatal mistake. There are too many distractions in our world to rely on memory. Studies show that we have less than thirty minutes to write an important fact down before we forget it. Yet we all are guilty of trusting our brains instead of our written word. Be smart—write it down so you can recall it later.

Sloppy follow-up is like burying your money in the backyard and forgetting where you buried it! You did all the work to earn the cash, and then you forgot where you hid it. The same is true with forgetting to follow up on a regular basis. Your relationship investment is lost because you forgot where you left it.

One of my favorite comments is "Mr. Jones, you can set your watch by me." With rock solid record keeping systems (computerized or manual), this should be our goal. Without it, we will lose what we have worked so hard to earn.

Creative Touches

We've discussed some of the more popular touches. I recommend all of them as part of your campaign. However, this is your relationship campaign, so the touches you use must reflect your style and personality to be effective.

I'm flattered when I see one of my former staff members or seminar attendees use one of my examples in their daily lives. What gets me more excited is watching someone take my ideas and make them their own. What about your business is different? What makes you different? What is unique about your background, your family, your education, and your hobbies? Use this information to create special touches.

Most of my business career was spent in Chicago. During a period of five years, the Chicago Bulls basketball team was the best in the world. The Windy City loved the Bulls, and you would be hard pressed to find anyone within a hundred miles of Chicago who did not know Michael Jordan and his team.

I remember a particular professional relationship builder who would send interesting information about the Bulls with his business card. This touch always had some interesting yet obscure fact about the team or a player. I loved receiving this quarterly touch. I found out later that this guy sent out over five hundred of these fact sheets to business professionals throughout the area.

Creativity in developing touches only multiplies your success. Creativity has a second advantage. It recharges the professional relationship process that can sometimes get dull and mundane. Doing the same things over and over again gets old. When activities get old, they don't get done. Without the regular scheduled touch, the relationship will die.

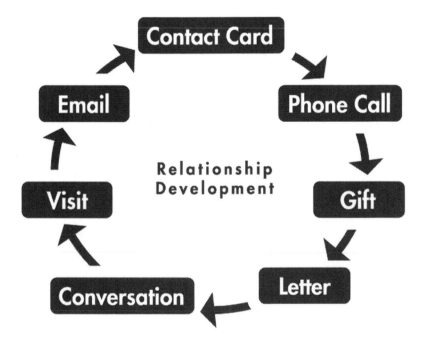

Studies show we must "touch" someone at least seven times before we can establish early levels of trust (relationship).

Building Relationships That Last A Lifetime

This is a relationship circle campaign. You can change the touches as you go round and round, remembering that we need to stay in touch to be successful. Touches work best when they are different and creative, based on the individual they are meant for.

Evaluating Progress

Once we start a relationship with an introduction, we decide whether or not we want a relationship with this individual. Over time, it makes sense to evaluate our progress with all our relationships and ask ourselves some questions and draw some conclusions.

Is the amount of time and effort invested in this relationship worth it?

Every relationship has its ups and downs. We are the only ones who can decide if the time and effort is worth it. Remember that some relationships will require more of us than we will ever get in return. These "service-based" relationships may require a lot of time and effort, but they can also be some of the most satisfying and enduring relationships, so we must be careful in our evaluation.

What can I do during my next touches to improve the relationship?

Every relationship can get better. What are we willing to do to improve our relationship with a contact? One simple way to make a huge difference is by asking the other person what can be done. This is a powerful touch and can tell us more about our relationship in twenty minutes than we have learned in years. Remember, you must have the other person's trust (no less than seven touches and maybe more) before you can expect a straight answer to this question.

The other person really does not seem to want a relationship with me.

No problem. If you have sincerely given your best effort to establish a relationship with someone and are continually rejected (I like three strikes), then say good-bye for good.

I want to be careful at this point, however, and make sure you are not taking the easy road. It's easy to flip off someone who rejects you at first blush. There are so many jokers running around this world trying to manipulate people that we all are very suspicious of someone who wants to "build a long-lasting relationship" with us. Don't be surprised if you get a lot of rejection in response to your noble intentions. Be polite, thorough, and firm. With experience you will win far more than you lose.

If a potential relationship looks valuable to your organization and you just can't break through, have someone else on your team give the relationship a try. Personal chemistry is very important in building relationships. Perhaps your chemistry just isn't what the other guy is looking for, so change the players and see what happens.

Regardless of the relationship type, the relationship circle makes sense. Too many times we leave the relationship touches and action points to someone else, and we wonder why things never quite work out. The reason is simple: we received what we planned and worked for.

Take some time and build your own sample campaign specific to your business or another type of relationship. Remember, develop at least seven touches before you present a proposal or ask the client or other person you are building a relationship with to do something, and always end a step by scheduling the next one. Your touches are designed to develop trust, so build on each contact.

If we want relationships that last a lifetime, then we must be willing to commit to the relationship circle and the effort it demands. By organizing our efforts into a well-designed campaign, our odds of success are stronger. If we rely on chance and good luck, building lasting relationships will be highly unlikely.

7.

The Power of Relationship Profiles

So far we have talked about types of relationships, compared them to farming, learned ways to bend dead-end straight lines into networked relationship circles, and described and illustrated numerous ways to reach out and touch someone, all of which is done for the sincere purpose of building trust and thus a relationship that lasts for a lifetime. Doing business or tackling a project together comes only after mutual trust is established. Time and diligent effort is required to pay attention to details and write things down, but this provides a wealth of important information about the people whom we are getting to know. How do we organize all of this information? One way is to create a client data sheet or a profile.

What Is a Profile?

A profile is an organized collection of information about an individual that is updated and expanded every time the individual is touched. This information is always taken down in writing and filed so later it can be easily retrieved.

A basic profile consists of all the usual contact information:

1. Name
2. Address
3. Telephone number
4. E-mail address
5. Employer
6. Job title
7. Job description

Keeping basic versions of a profile can be as simple as writing the info on a three-by-five-inch index cards and storing them alphabetically in a box or using a Rolodex (see chapter 10). These systems are better than none at all, yet the speed of business requires new systems and is moving faster than ever with mobile technology and cloud computing.

There are numerous customer relationship management (CRM) software tools such as Zoho CRM or web-based tools such as Salesforce.com to organize profile data and more. Some CRM systems are overkill but with proper training may be appropriate for certain businesses. Business contact management software can also work well whether you're using Microsoft Outlook, Mac Address Book, or a web-based system such as Google Contacts. Being able to sync information to laptops or mobile devices via cloud technology is an added time-saver and convenience. Whatever system you decide to use, the point is that we need more information in our client profiles than just the basics to build relationships that last a lifetime.

As we have discussed in previous chapters, the level of relationship we wish to achieve with any individual depends on how well we know them. To know someone well we must carefully and methodically collect and store information about the individual. To be effective in this important activity, we need to develop a detailed profile. Today's salespeople may be wired in a way that was never possible in bygone days, but to have good information always at your fingertips requires the same diligence in keeping your profiles up to date.

More Than Just a Form

If we start with the basic contact information (date, name, address, etc.) we have about 25 percent of a good profile sheet. The key to a good profile is a special field of information that we gather and use to develop a close relationship with a person. Unique items like college, hobbies and charitable involvement are special areas that take our relationships deeper and can yield fantastic results. Start with the contact basics, but build your profiles with each contact made so your profiles become loaded with special "touch points" unique to the individual.

Too Much Information?

There is never too much information in a profile. A good rule of thumb is one page of new information or the equivalent in keyed info for every year of time invested into building the relationship. If we have been building relationship with someone for five years, we should have five pages of profile information, meeting notes, relationship circle campaigns, and the like. Imagine how well we can serve an individual when we have five pages of information about them, their family, and their interests. Remember, it's about them.

Birthdays, Anniversaries, and Other Important Dates

One of the best days to talk to anyone is on their birthday. Unfortunately, most people do not know the birthdays of their relationships. Every profile form should include a section on important days. A specific type of birthday card (based on the individual) is always a welcome sight. Birthdays are also easy to track because they never change.

Anniversaries and other important dates in the lives of our relationships are also important. If a person mentions a date, then it's important and you need to keep track of it. The whole premise of a relationship circle is based on dates. Every time we complete a contact with a relationship, we schedule another one. Remember to think circles, not start-and-stop straight lines. Every action step should have a date when we will complete it, and our profile sheets should have plenty of such dates.

Important dates to remember can also come from the relationship's family and friends. A spouse's birthday, child's graduation, promotion date, or big project deadline all provide opportunities for personalized touches in the form of a simple card, phone call, or other acknowledgement and can make a huge impact on a relationship.

Profile a Company or Organization

It is important to profile individuals, but you can also profile a company. When profiling a company, one of the best tools is an organizational chart. These diagrams are usually a pyramid of connected boxes with the president on the top of the chart and all of the vice presidents, department managers, and supervisors below. Once you have the organizational chart completed, you can build individual profiles.

Combining company and individual profiles can be a very powerful tool for building business relationships. With enough information gathering and solid organization of that data, professional relationship builders can build complex profiles highlighting the interactions of departments, decision-making patterns, and much more. These power profiles become the building blocks in constructing a relationship with not only individuals, but the entire company. Many relationship development campaigns will overlap with other such campaigns inside the same client company, so make sure your profiles reflect contacts connected in one or more relationship campaigns.

A good file and retrieval system is critical as you build a profile on a company. Whether you prefer to use a computer or a well-organized file cabinet, the key to success is repetition. Every contact requires an update to the file. If there was one hundred touches to a relationship, there should be at least one hundred updates to the relationship file. Relying on your memory or the memory of others will cost you money, time, and your reputation as a professional relationship builder. Never complete a touch without an update to the file on what new information you learned, and when, what, and where the next touch will occur.

Every time the client is touched by your organization, it must be recorded in a central relationship filing system. Management should be able to access and review any client contact at any time and understand exactly what relationship work has been done over the years and which member of the company did the relationship work. Relationship managers can track the development of a firm's entire program by regularly reviewing the touch database. If a client has not been touched on a regular basis, odds are they are no longer a client.

There can be no black holes of information locked away in a remote file cabinet or personal computer. All contact management systems should be the same and integrated to prevent redundancy and overlap. If you are part of a relationship development team, your group should review your profile forms and processes at least once a year. Look at each other's data collection techniques and use the best practices as your standards. Teach the standards to everyone in the relationship development business (that's more than just the sales team), and integrate all profiled relationships into a central system.

Building Relationships That Last A Lifetime

Collect data as a group, but build the relationships on an individual basis.

There is nothing more embarrassing than having two relationship builders from the same company calling on the same client contact and not knowing it. Yet it happens too often in many good firms because relationships are not tracked and managed throughout the company. With good systems and standards in place, anyone in the company can quickly check a potential contact name and company to see if someone is "developing" a relationship with them as a representative of the company before an embarrassing double contact occurs. With proper security and training, most anyone in the company can check a good relationship development system to make sure everyone is on the same page when it comes to a business development contact.

Well-designed and maintained relationships database systems also help prevent the "bus factor." The bus factor happens when a relationship developer leaves the organization. "They were hit by a bus" is the way the impact of this change is described by those who are left to pick up where "the departed" left off. Another team member must pick up the relationship development effort quickly and painlessly. This is impossible without good profiling systems. The new guy should be able to pick up the touch campaign right where the old developer left off by reviewing the relationship file and touch campaign notes and data.

If the turnover is a planned activity, then a transition plan from one developer to another must be put in place. The old dog introduces the new dog to the relationship, and a new relationship begins. Hopefully, the new guy can earn back the trust of his predecessor.

Well-designed profile systems are true gold mines for the organizations that take the time, effort, and expense to operate them. Systems alone will not produce profitable relationship results. This requires well-trained people, operational and technical systems that support the relationship circle, and the discipline of everyone involved to do the work correctly.

When client relationships are touched, the records must reflect it immediately. If you are the person initiating the touch or taking the call, you carry the responsibility of updating the profile or seeing that the update is done accurately and in a timely fashion. Concentrate on the details across your organization, and big things will happen when it comes to your client relationships.

If you are a member of senior management, take time to see how your business relationships are located, created, and maintained. These business development activities are the lifeblood of your company. There are few organizations that neglect client relationships and survive. Make sure yours is not one of them.

A simple test for trouble is a profile review. Ask your development team to show you the profiles of your fifty largest customers. These files should be as thick as a telephone book with hundreds of contacts, meeting notes, organizational charts, and proposals. If your development team gives you a funny look or hands you a few sheets of paper with a few names and addresses on it, you have a problem.

As an organization, your team should have huge files on your top clients and prospects. Every decision maker's name, contact information, ninety-day project priority list, children's names, decision tree, and many other key information items should be complete, organized, and easily accessible. Multiply that information times one hundred, or even one thousand and you can see the size, scope, and importance of your professional relationship development systems.

These processes and systems are critical to any organization's survival. Top management must review this activity on a regular basis to insure the company's client relationships are being developed, maintained, and grown to insure the company's credibility based on earned trust as well as the financial future of the entire enterprise.

Knowledge Is Power

As you develop your profiles keep in mind the old saying "Knowledge is power." Gathering knowledge about our relationships by asking questions and recording what we learn is the building block of relationships. To achieve success, we must be more interested in learning about our contacts than we are in talking about ourselves. By showing a genuine interest in people, taking tedious notes, organizing the information, and responding in a timely fashion, we can serve people better. Relying on our memory, dealing with uncomfortable surprises, and plain missing the mark will only show our relationships that we are really not interested in them and just trying to manipulate and control relationships for our own selfish reasons.

When organizations are having poor sales performance, one of the first places to find problems is the prospect profile. If the quantity and content of the documentation are poor, you can bet your bottom dollar the sales numbers are worst. A lack of knowledge always equals a lack of sales. How can anyone expect to close business when they have too few prospects, little or no information about the prospects they do have, or no idea who the buyers really are within the target market?

The Chameleon Effect

A chameleon is a reptile that can change its color to match its environment. Place the creature on a green leaf, and the lizard will turn green. Then on a brown stick, and it will turn brown. Building relationships that last a lifetime requires a little of the chameleon effect.

When we seek to serve others, we need to adapt to their environment. If they wear jeans, we should consider wearing them too. If they are more formal in their attire, then we should wear a tie. The bottom line always comes down to serving them verses serving us. We should emulate their mode of operation as much as possible. If we are serious about building relationships, then it's up to us to meet people where they are. When we set aside our arrogance, we build comfort. Comfort opens the door to relationship and makes trust a real possibility.

In the computer consulting business, we would stress the importance of our people "joining" the client's team. When I would tour the client's offices, it should be difficult to spot our consultants among the client's full-time employees. They are a team, and no longer two different groups. Even though we had an extensive computer lab at our offices, we always wanted our people working at the client site as often as possible. If we needed our computer facilities, then we would invite the client to come and use our offices as well. If the client's full-time staff started work at 8:00, our people started at 8:00. If they wore suits and ties to work, we wore suit and ties as well.

Regardless of what your company does or makes, *every* company is in the service business. Your service may be selling cars, a doctor's office, or a pizza stand—all are service companies first! Every successful company in the world is a service company. We may make tires, but service is what we do.

Are your personal and business objectives service? Or are you trying to sell something? Serve first, sell second, and you will never be disappointed with the results.

May I Take a Few Notes?

There are few questions more important in the world of professional relationship builders than this one: "May I take a few notes while we talk?" When someone asks this question of me, I not only feel that the person talking to me thinks I'm important, but I think he's a real professional and serious about our time together.

Always have your journal and pen at the ready when you are speaking with someone whom you wish to build a long-term relationship with. You never know when an important piece of information may pop up. Without good notes, you will forget.

Having a copy of the individual's profile sheet is also very helpful. You can update the information and make a permanent change when you are finished with your conversation. Once again, it shows a high level of professionalism when you ask to confirm contact information. Also, changes to old information can be a signal that something new is happening in the life of your contact.

No matter how excellent it may be, do not rely on your memory when talking with client contacts. It will always fail you. The small piece of information you miss may cost you the relationship someday, so always be ready to write it down in a spiral notebook not easily removed or lost.

If I really want the information, then I should be willing to burn through a box of pens and a case of spiral notebooks to do it. Plus, I believe that writing by hand, or even keyboarding, stimulates the mind and keeps us sharp when talking with others. There is nothing wrong with using a laptop, tablet, or similar devices for note taking during a conversation. Just be careful the person you're meeting with does not find this method uncomfortable and stop talking. Whether you use a pen or a PC, just make sure it does not stand in the way of a good conversation. Once you practice a little, taking notes during conversation will become second nature.

An example of a profile form appears on the following page. There are no right or wrong fields for your personal system. The more you know, the stronger the relationship potential. If possible talk with your team and get consensus on what information is important to track and develop. Review your profile form at least once a year to make sure it still fits your business needs. Nothing stays the same for long, so review your forms and systems on a regular basis.

When you look at this sample profile form, you see the obvious information blanks such as name and address. What makes a profile form powerful are the special fields such as "Hobbies" and "Favorite sports." Collecting this type of data on a relationship sets us apart from just another person. People love to talk about their favorite topic—themselves. We need

Building Relationships That Last A Lifetime

Sample Profile Form

Name: _____ Last touched: _____

Address: _____

City: _____ State: _____ Zip: _____

E-mail: _____

Business phone: _____ Home phone: _____

Cell: _____ Other: _____

Company: _____

Duties: _____

Assistant: _____ Telephone: _____

Key Staff Members: _____

Dates: _____ Top projects in 90 days: _____

Touch 1 (date): _____ Touch 4 (date): _____

Touch 2 (date): _____ Touch 5 (date): _____

Touch 3 (date): _____ Touch 6 (date): _____

Hobbies: _____ College: _____

Birthday: _____ Spouse: _____

Children: _____ Grandchildren: _____

Favorite sports: _____

Sports played: _____

Referred by: _____

to design data collection and retrieval systems that allow us to collect each piece of special information on our relationships. The profile form is the most basic.

Back before laptops and tablet computers, it was difficult to carry several hundred profile sheets with you as you went about your day. Those days are long gone. Handheld devices can bring up all your profile data with a few swipes or taps of your finger, yet some people may prefer good ole paper and pen. So if you do not carry your relationship profiles with you, you need to take a copy or condensed version with you prior to engaging a contact.

Have your profile information with you when you contact your client. Review your material *before* you "touch" the contact. Know what new information you need to gather, and work the appropriate questions into your conversation.

Preparation is one of the most important areas when it comes to follow-up. Why are you meeting with this person? What did you talk about last time? Did you promise to prepare or bring some information of value for the contact? What interesting item can you leave with them after the meeting? These and other questions must be asked and reviewed *before* you make the next contact. As always, be sure to listen first, yet also have an agenda for your touch. Even if you are only touching base, ask a few more questions about the individual and add this new data to your profile. Make each contact count!

When you meet someone for the first time, you may find it difficult to gather a lot of personal information. That's fine, because a good profile sheet may take years to complete. The stronger your relationship becomes, the more comfortable you will feel about asking questions about someone's family, hobbies, or life stories. Take your time. Relationship building naturally takes time.

Every touch *must* be recorded and the next touch scheduled. Remember, we are thinking circles and not straight lines. Our profile forms, databases, and calendaring devices must all compliment the relationship circle. We *never* let someone slip through the cracks.

Developing a good profile form for personal or business use may take some time. Don't be afraid to change the form and add new fields. Each professional industry will have unique fields of jargon specialized for their marketplace. If this is true in your profession, by all means, make sure it is represented in your profiles.

Building Relationships That Last A Lifetime

As mentioned in chapter 5, a good relationship builder should have one page of profile information or an equivalent amount of keyed information about a relationship for every year of building that relationship. A five-year professional relationship should have a nice, thick profile with data sheets, client company brochures, organizational charts, decision tree charts, and lots of profile notes.

Track Important Client Projects and Deadlines

Using your profile data sheets to track a client's projects is one of the best ways to win business. Every touch with a business relationship should include this question: "What projects, activities, or events are critical for you and your department over the next ninety days, and how can I help you get them done successfully?"

A typical business relationship will have several answers to this important question. Make sure you have them all listed, prioritized, and dated so your follow-up and future touches serve these important activities of your client. When you make the next follow-up touch, it should include ideas, products, or information that help the prospect or client with their important projects. Otherwise, how can you serve someone when you don't know what's important to them over the next three months?

Simple small talk will grow old if you do not bring value to your business touches. People expect something for their time, and we need to deliver with information, products, and services that help them get their big projects completed if we want to build a strong business relationship. Everything we do as professional relationship builders should help our contacts achieve those important "to-do" items on their list. Not only do we ask about them every time we touch, but we must offer real-world help to get these activities done on time and on budget. If our products or services can help, great; if not, we need to assist our business relationship by connecting them with other contacts and vendors who can bring assistance and value to the project.

If you have major business relationships and do not know their top priorities over the next ninety days, you are missing the boat. We need to ask, update, and track these important projects on a regular basis if we are serious about building a lifelong relationship. Your profile should be more that just a couple of data sheets and a few scattered notes. Your systems should resemble an organized tracking system. To be effective, your systems must not only track the individual, but their projects and activities as well. Any information about the individual, company, products, or news articles should be kept organized in the file for easy access and reviewed and updated constantly. There is nothing worst than missing a big news article on your largest client and having them ask you if you saw it.

Many large organizations engage clipping firms to keep track of news articles about their clients. Thousands of dollars are spent annually on such services because they work. As you read specific industry material related to your business relationships, watch for interesting articles. Get copies or reprints made and give them to related relationships. People love to read about their company or industry, so make an effort to collect industry information and share it with your prospects and clients. These articles make fantastic touches.

Develop your profile forms, collect and maintain good information about your professional relationships including those key projects, and good things will happen to your sales numbers. Sync your profiles with your relationship circle, and make sure your touches and collection methods work together. Each touch should increase information in the profile.

Now that we have a profile system in place, the next step is to organize our information so we can access it quickly and efficiently. It's time to develop a database.

8.

Organized Profiles = Database

Professional relationship builders keep a large collection of contacts, employees, customers, friends, and prospects. If you are in the sales profession, you should have hundreds, if not thousands, of contacts who are in various stages of relationship development.

How do you keep all of this information in good working order? You use a well-organized filling system also known as a database. The word *database* is often a misunderstood concept. A database is a file system organized in some logical manner. It may be alphabetical, numeric, or by several other criteria. The organization and ease of retrieval makes a good database a must-have for serious relationship builders.

Whether the system is hosted on a supercomputer or is as simple as a box full of three-by-five-inch index cards, both are database systems. As we look at our relationship profiles, touch circles, and information files, organizing them is a top priority if we want our information to work for us in building relationships. But one of the best ways to get started or to update an old database system is IBM.

IBM

IBM stands for: **I**t's **B**etter **M**anually.

Here is how it works. Lay out all of your written information for one relationship. What do you have? If you have been following some of the suggestions outlined in this book, here are a handful of things you should have:

1. *A relationship profile* with one page of information or the equivalent in keyed info for every year of development
2. *A touch circle campaign* with your ongoing touches outlined and planned
3. *A calendar* with daily scheduled touches and follow-up activities
4. *A personal journal* with your to-do lists
5. *An information file* for each relationship that is important to you or your organization, including an annual report, organizational chart, and any other information about the company or its products.

Now that we have all the key sources of data in front of us, let's put them in a system that makes sense. As we organize our information, it's important to use common sense. Too many times, however, organizations rush to technology for the sake of mere organization or powerful features. There is nothing more costly or destructive than automating a poor process. Take a moment and do a little drawing.

In a business setting, call a meeting of the key relationship builders in your company. Once together, document the relationship-building process that is most effective. The picture created should look like a circle. Document each step from a cold call to an information file to a contact management system. Look for common ground so everyone can use a similar if not the same system. Remember, the more people can agree on a process, the more powerful the process becomes.

Once the group has agreed to a relationship development process, then systems can be discussed that best serve the process. It's just that simple. The best process may be a manual file system done well and updated often, or it may be a sophisticated computer database costing millions. Both require the same effort in terms of design, planning, and standards to be effective.

Human Touch in a High-Tech World

Computers are awesome tools and can multiply our productivity in building relationships. The danger with technologically enhanced productivity is the removal of human contact from the relationship-building process in favor of computerized touches.

The use of sophisticated CRM (customer relationship management) technology to build relationships cannot replace people. CRM software like that mentioned in chapter 7 may be able to facilitate relationship-building efforts such as automated form letters, voice mail messages, e-mails, podcasts, and worldwide teleconferences, but they cannot cement a relationship like a handshake.

The more advanced our tools become, the less personal our approach. If we really appreciate the power of solid relationships, then we must be on guard to keep our contacts as personal as possible. Technology is great, but it does not build relationships. People do that.

Some of the best relationship databases are a combination of computer and manual systems. At BALR Corporation, all of our relationship builders carried a basic set of tools with them at all times:

- A cell phone
- A spiral notebook personal journal
- A calendaring device
  (Day-Timer, Franklin, or PDA with at least one-year capabilities)
- A business card (more than a few)

When the team returned from the field, they had several more tools at their disposal. Our company maintained a contact database of clients, prospects, and follow-up activities. We also kept a detailed information file of client literature, organization charts, and customer product literature. This filed information was important for any consultant or new team member who was assigned to a known customer of prospect. They could simply spend some time with the file and learn a good deal about the company and people they would be working with.

To determine if your database system is working properly, do a random audit. Pick a dozen prospects at random that are not doing any business with your firm currently. Ask the relationship developer in charge of those contacts to tell you something about the prospect. If this task is difficult or inaccurate, you have a problem.

If your company needs thousands of prospects to make a profit, then you should have thousands of prospect profiles in various phases of development. These campaigns must be organized, planned, and worked if any business is ever going to happen.

How many relationships do you need to be successful in your professional, personal, family, and spiritual life? Would fifty, one hundred, five hundred, or even a thousand different relationships be sufficient? The larger that number, the more complete the filing and recall process must be.

Common Sense = Simple System + Discipline

Step back from your current systems and take a fresh look. With the relationship circle in mind, review each step in entering, reviewing, and retrieving your relationship information. Does it work? Does it make sense? What areas can be improved? Does a system even exist? Do not rely on your memory.

Doing all the work required to build powerful relationships is wasted in an instant when we forget. Relying on memory to follow up, get requested information, or reply to a question destroys relationships. Reliance on memory and poor note taking has cost businesses millions of dollars in lost opportunities. Use database systems to eliminate the need for human memory. No matter how good your memory may be, you will forget some date, detail, or fact, and it will be a painful reminder why we need good systems to keep relationship information.

Good business process, good computer system.

Bad business process, deadly computer system.

Remember, our goal is to continually touch people on a regular basis. Each touch yields more and more information about the contact. This knowledge becomes power as we use it to serve the needs of our relationships. Spread over years, this ongoing activity becomes a powerful and profitable part of our professional and personal lives.

The database system keeps all of this history and data organized and on schedule. You do not need millions of dollars to utilize many of these exciting new data retrieval systems. However, you do need common sense. Always challenge the norm and keep your relationship information and follow-up a high priority. Most of all, keep the process as simple as possible, always seeking to improve it.

A good database system makes sense for more than just business relationships. How many times have we forgotten a birthday, anniversary, or other important event? This simple information could be tracked with a pocket calendar, PDA, or other calendaring system. There is no excuse not to have this information readily available. If we value the relationship, then we must value the data, dates, and information that pertain to it. Forgetting dates, appointments, and other important events is simply a lack of having a simple system and the discipline to use it without fail. Forgetting simply says, "I'm not really interested in you."

Taking your profile information to the next level using a database is a great idea. There are no simple answers in automating this process. Proceed slowly remembering that the computer supports the profile process and not the other way around.

If we keep our information on a computer, then how do we take it with us? Obviously mobile technology is one answer to this question. But be careful not to chain yourself to your desk or even to your tablet for every piece of relationship data you need. Think about your daily routine and what systems make sense for you. One size does not fit all, so take the time to select products and techniques that make sense.

Touching people on a regular, scheduled basis with a plan of building relationships that last a lifetime is not rocket science, but it does require simple systems and the discipline to use them every day.

9.

How to Build a Relationship Development Campaign

Now that we have covered all of the individual pieces required to build relationships, let's bring them all together into a campaign. Although all relationships could utilize a development campaign, we will focus on a new business relationship for this example.

Before we can develop a business relationship campaign, we need to identify the individual or company that we will attempt to reach and establish a working relationship with. Market research is critical to save time and effort. There is no reason to attempt relationship building with an individual or company that has no need of our service or product. As discussed in previous chapters, a local library is a great place to identify business clients. We will talk more about researching clients in the next chapter.

Once our research and identification homework is completed, we can design a relationship campaign. We start the campaign with a blank relationship circle. In a campaign, we want to touch the potential client at least seven times before we ask for any type of sale or commitment. With this in mind, we need seven touch activities outlined on our circle before we present our product or service.

First Touch

The first touch box is the introduction touch. There are many ways to contact a potential business relationship for the first time. For our example, we will use a letter. The introduction letter is a brief text introducing us and our organization. The letter should be no more than one page and highlight the advantages of the organization and the next step in the process. The next step is a telephone follow-up call.

With research done in advance, all basic contact information is ready for the letter and profile form. Key contacts, address, company location, and product line are all easily accessible through the Internet. The more we know in advance, the more successful our relationship development will be. Do your homework first!

An investigative telephone call to the prospect before you send the introduction letter is another way to further refine your information. Talking to a receptionist, secretary, or a security guard can provide valuable information. Be careful not to talk to your target person until you have sent the introduction letter.

Making a telephone call without any preparation work or introduction mailing is called a cold call. The reason this shot in the dark is called a cold call is the typical response you get from the prospect on the other end of the call. A very cold one! There is nothing wrong with calling, but it is very difficult to establish a professional relationship by using this technique. Remember, the straight-line mess? Cold calls are perfect examples of straight-line "yes" or "no" actions.

When a prospect is contacted with no advanced warning, the surprise factor usually results in a negative response. By contrast, a well-written introduction letter will suggest a follow-up step. Enclose your card and a simple company brochure. Do not send anything expensive in this first touch; it may end up in the trashcan. A company pen or another small giveaway item is a nice addition to this early touch.

A good follow-up step after an introduction letter is a telephone call. Use the last paragraph of your letter to announce your upcoming telephone call intentions: "I will contact you next week to answer any questions you may have and learn more about you, your organization, and how we can work together in the future. I look forward to talking with you."

Make a note in your personal calendaring device to follow up with a telephone call. Before your touch is completed, start your profile form and contact file with all the information you have uncovered to date. Don't leave anything out, since this early information will be the foundation of all future touches and activities. Important items such as name, address, title, company name, product lines, and several other key pieces of information should be obtained. Make sure you get all of this information documented in your profile form and review it. Never contact a business customer without reviewing your profile and contact information first. Being informed and organized makes a huge impression. If the target company is public, you can get a copy of their annual report and tons of information from their public relations department or their website.

The contact file is complete for your first contact when you have finished the following items:

1. *A profile form* with all the basic information completed
2. *A copy of the letter sent to the contact* with the upcoming telephone call highlighted
3. *An entry in your calendaring device* for the day, time, and subject of your next touch
4. *Any contact database entry* starting the computer file on this contact and company
5. *A contact file* containing all research information on the contact, company, and their products or services such as annual reports and copies of their website information.

Second Touch

Once an introduction package has been sent, the next step in building this business relationship is the follow-up phone call. We mentioned this call in our introduction letter, so we need to make the call precisely when we said we would.

Making the first telephone call to a new contact can be difficult. Many prospects employ an entire staff of call screeners. These individuals will make it tough to actually talk to the decision makers. Regardless, always be polite and to the point when using the telephone. Simply ask for your contact in a professional manner and voice. If asked the nature of your call, tell the screener that materials were sent to "Mr. Jones" (use Mr. or Ms. and last name) and you were following up to answer questions and provide additional data. The more professional and organized your call appears to the screener, the better your chances of being connected.

91

Most larger companies receive hundreds of "follow-up calls" each week, so don't be surprised if the call screener is a little grumpy. You may need a couple of calls before you actually reach your prospect. Don't worry, it happens to the best of us.

Once connected, we may hit another call screening system—the dreaded voice mail. Do not hang up; it's time for another touch. A voice mail message counts as your second touch, so make it count. Practice leaving a voice mail message for your new contact before you make this phone call. It is an important part of a relationship builder's skill set, and practice makes perfect. For those who need extra work developing your phone voice, a tape recorder is an excellent way to practice (for more on this, see chapter 6).

Leave a short voice mail message telling your prospect why you are calling.

> *Mr. Jones, this is Ron Rice. I'm following up on an information package I sent you last week. I wanted to answer any questions you may have about our company, and how we can help you and your team in the future. I will try to reach you later today and arrange a good time to talk further. I look forward to meeting you and earning your business.*

There are many different styles and methods in leaving voice mail messages. Make sure you are comfortable with this medium and your message.

Many executives use voice mail to screen their calls. Some never answer their phone and prefer to listen to voice mail and return calls that are of interest to them. So if you want a return call, leave a solid, well-thought-out message.

If the first call ends up with your prospect's assistant, the same type of message is warranted. Don't go into great detail, but give the assistant enough information to show you mean business. Make sure you inform the message taker that you will call back if you do not hear from your contact. You can even ask the message taker when a good time is to catch your contact at their desk: "Is Mr. Jones a morning person, or does he return most of his calls in the afternoon?"

Once a good message is delivered, a second attempt can be made within twenty-four hours. If that attempt is unsuccessful, then try again in three days.

Building Relationships That Last A Lifetime

Make sure the profile system is updated with each attempt. If the contact has an assistant, make sure you get that person's name in the profile. A professional assistant can be your greatest ally or your worst nightmare, so make sure you handle them correctly. The assistant should be on your radar as another person with whom to develop a relationship as well as their boss. Remember, at least seven touches before you establish trust.

If three messages do not yield a return call, it's time for another letter. The second letter outlines the attempts made to contact the individual. Keep the letter positive and upbeat. Remember, we are serving them and not vice versa.

There are many reasons why the contact may not return your calls. Some are legitimate and some are not. It's up to you how much of your valuable time you want to spend with someone who does not seem interested. My personal rule was always three attempts to connect, and then move on. If you still believe the contact is someone you would like to have as a business relationship, make a note to start the entire process over again in three months.

After three months has passed, send the person another introduction letter as if they were a brand-new contact. Don't change a thing. If the first letter was screened, the contact may have never seen your first letter, so in their eyes this is the first contact. My introduction campaign was rejected for five years by one of my largest customers. I knew they would make a great business relationship if I could ever break through. I kept restarting every six months, and it finally paid off.

Of course we realize that turnabout is fair play. Salespeople tried to reach me as head of my organization's sales department, so our receptionist would screen their calls just like my calls were screened calling future clients. There was a certain salesman who wanted to come in and talk to me about their line of giveaway doodads. They sold pens, mugs, golf balls, shirts, you name it. Their catalog was three inches thick!

After repeated attempts, this clever relationship builder started sending me interesting greeting cards in the mail addressed and written by hand. I remember one with a funny looking dragon breathing fire. The caption was, "It's a real Dragon not getting to speak with you." Pretty corny I thought, but there were several others that arrived about once a month.

Finally, I took a telephone call and complimented the salesman on his mail and card campaign. He thanked me and asked if I would go one step further and meet with him. I agreed and his company became a loyal and trusted vendor over many years. Most of our best giveaways came from this company. When we needed something different or special, Gary always had an idea. My only regret was not recruiting him to work for us. He knew how to build relationships and was very successful.

What happens if you actually get to talk to your contact on your first call? The first follow-up call should be about the contact, and not about you. Have a series of questions ready so you can learn as much about the contact as possible. Do not take more time than the contact is willing to give in the first follow-up conversation. Ten to twenty minutes for the first call is good. The first telephone conversation is just a touch and not an in-depth interview.

If you sense a good chemistry during your first telephone call, suggest a face-to-face meeting to explore ideas in more detail. By taking fantastic notes during your phone conversation, you have an agenda for your first meeting staring you in the face. Take the top priority items for the prospect and make them your agenda for your first visit. Remember, we have only two touches under our belts at this point, so resist the temptation to ask for a deal or to pitch an idea. We are still building trust with our new business relationship.

If the new relationship asks for information about us or our company, give it to them, but in a very brief and professional manner. Watch your time, and don't get caught trying to sell something on the phone. Hit some high points about your organization. Your prospect may be testing you to see if you are a real professional or just another telemarketer. Don't forget the seven touches rule!

When the telephone conversation goes well, ask the contact for some time to meet in person and spend some quality time together. If the prospect declines a meeting, that's okay. Schedule a follow-up telephone call in a couple of weeks to take the information-gathering process to the next step.

There is nothing wrong with tracking the client over the telephone until there is a need to sit down and have a deeper level of conversation. Each call generates more information and more trust. Be mindful of the client's upcoming projects and challenges so you are ready to move forward when they are. I had several clients who loved to talk on the phone but shied away from face-to-face meetings. It's about the client's preferences, and not yours. Go with the flow.

Building Relationships That Last A Lifetime

After your first telephone conversation, you should have tons of new information about the prospect to enter into your client profile and database. Make sure you get all the information into your system as soon as possible. The more time that passes, the greater your chance of losing the data.

Third through Seventh Touches

Always send follow-up materials in the mail after a telephone conversation. These materials can be another letter thanking the prospect for their time. A business card, giveaway, brochure, relevant news article, book appropriate to contact's interests, or other tangible touches are all nice follow-ups. Send something that will not end up in the trashcan. This counts as touch number three!

Your next contact should be a visit or telephone meeting with an agenda. The prospect is starting to trust you, and you should be able to gather more and more information about the prospect, their company, and what important challenges they will be facing over the next ninety days. Your note-taking skills will determine how successful you are during this critical phase of business relationship development. Have your personal journal and a good pen ready and working overtime.

After your second telephone call, or your first face-to-face, you should have a solid idea where, when, and how your product or service can help the prospect achieve their goals. At this point in the relationship, you should have three or more calls, at least one face-to-face visit, and four follow-up mailings with giveaways. Take inventory on your touches so far. Do you have at least seven?

If you've done your relationship building homework, it should be obvious what product or service makes sense for this client. If the product or service fit is not clear, then you have some more questions to ask. Don't push products or services that don't make sense just to close a sale. You may win a battle, but you will lose a war. Patience is indispensable. It amazes me how many professional relationship builders will throw away months of hard work by trying to close a sale with a product or service that does not fit. Ask yourself a simple question: "If I was the client, would this offer be of value to me?"

Eighth Touch: A Written Proposal

Your written proposal or offer should be your eighth-touch minimum, never before that point in the relationship. Always propose a sale in writing.

Whether the deal is worth a hundred dollars or one hundred million dollars, always put your offer in writing. This is another touch toward trust.

When presenting your proposal, always give the client the opportunity to change the document. Get your clients involved in writing your proposals early and often as you approach a close. It's much easier to ask for a deal when the product or service was a team effort with both sides of the transaction playing an active role.

Several of our largest proposals were reworked several times as a group project. What started as my proposal became our proposal and closed with little effort. Once both sides have agreed to the language and terms of the proposal, the deal is closed. It's pretty tough for a client to turn down a proposal they wrote!

Congratulations! You built a solid working business relationship, provided a service or product to a customer who needed it, and hopefully made a few dollars of profit along the way. But the hardworking farmer's work is never done. Celebrate your success and then attend to your fields and next crop to insure a good harvest as well as future seasons of productive yields.

Follow-Up, Project Review, and Planning Next Steps

As the project is being developed or delivered, stay close to the action. Make sure everything is done as promised. There is nothing worse than not delivering what you promised. If it happens on a regular basis, you need to find another career, or another employer. There is nothing more important to your future as a professional relationship developer than your word. Defend it at all cost.

Once the project or product has been delivered and installed, its time for some quality assurance conversations. Sit down with the client and thank them for their business. During this conversation, pull out your journal and start asking questions about the entire relationship and the products or services delivered. "How did our people do?" "What could we do better next time?" "How was our proposal verses the actual final product?" These are all great questions. Develop your own questions based on your industry or area of business.

Once you have completed your Q&A, it's time to start the whole process over again. As you wrap up the Q&A meeting, your last question should be, "Let's get together in two weeks and start talking about what's next. How does Tuesday the 20th look, say 10 o'clock?" If you do your job well, the business relationship circle goes on for many years, many deals, and many profitable projects for everyone concerned.

Lay out a hypothetical relationship circle for your unique business. Include seven touches, a proposal or offer, a completed close, and quality assurance. Plan your campaigns based on your product or service and the potential clients who can use them. Revise your strategy based on feedback from your business relationships and you will have a powerful relationship methodology you can teach future employees.

A completed relationship development campaign can be illustrated for training purposes or for the benefit of visualizing the overall layout and steps in the relationship-building process. Since the example given is designed for a hypothetical company, the touch steps are generic. Use this diagram as a template for building campaigns unique to your business.

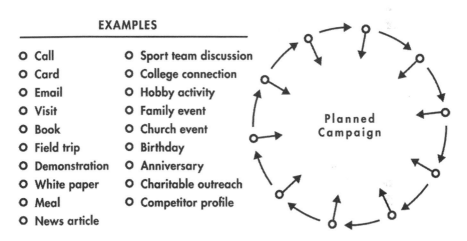

EXAMPLES	
O Call	O Sport team discussion
O Card	O College connection
O Email	O Hobby activity
O Visit	O Family event
O Book	O Church event
O Field trip	O Birthday
O Demonstration	O Anniversary
O White paper	O Charitable outreach
O Meal	O Competitor profile
O News article	

Planned Campaign

In a relationship campaign, every touch is targeted around one specific individual. Campaigns are unique. Tailor each relationship based on the person you are building the relationship with. This list is just to get you started.

Application and Discipline

"Knowledge without application is simply trivia."

I have outlined what it takes to build relationships that last a lifetime, but this knowledge is useless if we do not apply it! When I talk with most professionals having career trouble, the problem is usually based around two areas: application and discipline. Most people understand their jobs. They know how, why, and when to do all the functions required by their position, yet they fail. They have knowledge, but they have trouble applying what they know. This situation is usually a result of poor training or management.

Every person should start their day with a plan. Whether you are working or on vacation, a little organization helps you enjoy life. Even if your plan is to do nothing but nap, that's still a good plan! Without a plan, things do not get done. When activities don't get completed, nothing grows. When nothing grows, we waste time and eventually our life.

A daily plan is an application of what we know. Not planning is a lack of discipline. A volume of books could be written on the application of knowledge or on the discipline of success. To accomplish anything in our lives from learning to ride a bike to performing a heart transplant, application and discipline play a major role.

The same is true in building relationships that last a lifetime. The discipline to make the calls, to send the letters, to remember the birthdays, to always schedule the next contact, or to follow up on a brief introduction makes all the difference in the quality and quantity of our relationships.

Taking the time to apply what you have read and adapting it to your own circumstances is the only way these techniques can change your life. Just knowing them and understanding their significance is not enough. It is only by doing (application) certain activities every day (discipline) that things happen.

10.

The Power of People

As I travel around this great country of ours, people ask me on a regular basis what the secret to my success was. The answer to this question is a simple one: I have more relationships than most people, and those "contacts" made me a wealthy man.

In chapter 12, we will discuss towers and pyramids and why having a broad and deep client base will allow any organization to survive and flourish even in tough times. The same is true with your relationships. "It's not what you know, but who you know that will make you successful." I do not know who originally said this, but truer words were never spoken.

Since my early days of selling Kirby vacuum cleaners door-to-door, I've always been fascinated with people and what they did for a living. I've met thousands of interesting people from all walks of life, and had the ability to keep track of most of them throughout my professional career.

My Secret Weapon: The Rolodex

One of my "secret weapons" was the Rolodex. This simple rolling filing system has been a part of my life for over thirty years. I do not remember who started me collecting business cards, but I owe that person a tremendous debt of gratitude. Many people who have seen my collection think it is one of the largest in the world. Although I've cleaned it out a time or two, it still has thousands of cards.

When I encounter a challenging situation where the answer is in question, I simply go to the good old Rolodex and start spinning. For those of you who do not know what a Rolodex is, go ahead and Google it or just picture a three-by-five-inch index card with slots on the bottom. The card mounts to a cylinder via those slots. A large Rolodex can hold 250 of these index cards and can be turned by simply spinning the device by the ends. Take a business card and staple it to the blank index card and voilà! You have a powerful database of people right at your fingertips.

I filed my cards in alphabetical order, but occasionally by profession. Yesterday, I was looking for my fiberglass repairman and could not remember his name. Sure enough, I found his card under "F" for fiberglass.

Imagine how many people your have met in your life? Now imagine how large your Rolodex collection would be if each one had given you a business card? Unfortunately, some interesting people you will meet do not have a business card. No problem, simply make one for them in your Rolodex using the blank index card.

From Rolodex to Touching Base Regularly

If you think using a Rolodex is obsolete, it really doesn't have to be. Online social networks and technology that syncs all of our devices made their debut not all that long ago. The technology will continue to change, but what remains the same is that people still have relationship networks as they always have, and will use a mix of old and new ways to reach out and "touch" their contacts on a regular basis.

Find a way to organize your contact information that works well and use that info on a regular basis to build relationships. You can buy a card scanner to add business cards electronically or use a smartphone camera, which can be equipped with OCR (optical character recognition) apps to digitally convert printed business cards into contact cards that can become profiles and organized into a database.

As with any relationship, we must touch each contact in our "Rolodex" (whether on earth or in the cloud) if we want them to remain part of our lives. I found a simple letter once or twice a year very effective in maintaining contact.

Here is an example of such a letter:

Greetings Bill,
I hope this letter finds you and yours doing well.
Erin and I are still enjoying our semiretirement traveling the country

and spending our winters in Florida and our summers at Lake of the Ozarks. I'm still working on that book and doing a little consulting and staffing here and there.

I still keep your card in my Rolodex, and I value our relationship over the years. Please drop me a new card or letter if anything has changed in your contact information.

Continued success in all you pursue. Please feel free to call me anytime if I can be of service in any way.

Thank you for your friendship over the years, and I look forward to catching up with you soon.

Sincerely,

Ron

Ronald Rice

I send out thousands of these letters a year to keep my contact base as fresh as possible.

Imagine having the best lawyer, engineer, artist, writer, CEO, CFO, CMO, or CIO at your fingertips! That's what I have, and it's one of the reasons for my success. Some of my contacts were former clients, some former employees, and some even former competitors. All are there and ready for a phone call.

The Smartest Person on the Planet Is . . .

When Henry Ford was at the peak of his power and prestige, the *New York Times* sent a reporter to his office in Dearborn, Michigan, to interview the world's richest man. When the reporter arrived at Ford's office, he started the interview with an obvious question.

"Mr. Ford, what do you think is the number one reason why you have become so successful?"

Ford thought about the question for a moment, smiled, and replied: "That's easy son, I'm the world's smartest man!"

The young reporter squirmed in his chair a little and attempted to clarify the tycoon's response: "Well, Mr. Ford . . . You're a great industrialist, visionary inventor, world-class organizer, and a true visionary . . . but you really think you are the world's smartest man?"

Ford quickly responded: "Absolutely, no doubt about it . . . I am the world's smartest man. Go ahead . . . ask me any question . . . any topic . . . Please . . . Please . . . ask me any question," Ford challenged his young interviewer.

"Okay, Mr. Ford," the reporter began. "What is the relevance of Einstein's Theory of Relativity and its significance to modern man."

Ford stared blankly at the reporter and asked a clarification question. "That is a science question, right?" The reporter nodded in agreement. Mr. Ford reached across his desk and pushed his intercom box button buzzing his secretary. When she answered, Ford asked her to send in Johnson right away. Within a few minutes in walked a scholarly looking fellow dressed in a lab coat, pocket protector, glasses, and a very serious looking notebook.

"How may I help you, Mr. Ford?" the lab-coated visitor asked. Ford asked the reporter to restate his question. Within seconds, Johnson was at the chalk board, dissecting Einstein's theories in great detail and breaking down the key elements and why they apply not only to the automobile, but to our everyday lives. After forty-five minutes, a chalk-covered Johnson turned to his two-person audience and asked if there were any questions.

Ford turned to his interviewer and waited for any follow-up questions for the bespectacled scientist who stood before him. After a moment, the reporter smiled and said the answer was quite satisfactory. Ford thanked Johnson and sent him back to work.

"There you have it," said Ford. "Any other questions?"

The reporter protested, "Mr. Ford, you did not know all that information about Einstein's theories."

Ford smiled and ended the discussion with one final statement. "You are correct, young man, I did not know all that material on Einstein. I was smart enough to hire Mr. Johnson."

This story about Henry Ford drives home an important point for all of us. People are powerful assets if we take the time to engage them. Henry Ford hired many talented people to work for the Ford Motor Company and turned that team of talent into one of the world's greatest organizations.

You may never get a chance to hire a man like Mr. Johnson or a Henry Ford, but you will have a chance to meet men and woman of similar intelligence throughout your life. What you do with those encounters and what follow-up you initiate will determine the impact these meetings have in your life and on your career. Turn your meetings from straight lines that go nowhere into circles that keep these valuable contacts a part of your life.

You can be one of the smartest people on the planet simply by the people you know and stay in touch with. Just like me.

PART TWO

Building
a Great Company

ᎧᏚᏟᎡ

11.

How to Know Your Customers

Today, many people start their own business. New companies and the entre-preneurs who start them are driving most of the job growth around the world.

One of the early steps in launching a company, or improving an existing one is the process of looking at your marketplace. To get the best view of potential business relationships, you need to fly high and survey the potential farm fields before you bring out your tractor. (Yes, our farmer is at it again.)

To determine your marketplace, a few simple questions need to be asked and answered:

1. What is you product or service? *(Be specific.)*
2. What type of person or business would benefit from my product? *(Be specific.)*
3. How many customers would I need to be profitable? *(Do the numbers.)*
4. How many of my potential customer relationships are in my backyard, neighborhood, city, county, state, nation, and world? *(Start small and get large.)*

Focus

Asking questions is a good first step in the wide world of market research. The important thing to remember in the early stages of research is focus. Be as specific as possible about your product or service. Can you describe your product or service in one sentence?

Too many young companies fail because they try to be everything to everybody and end up serving no one. Choose your product or service wisely. Then test the market to see just how good or needed your idea will be. If the results of your research are less than exciting, enhance your product and try again.

Once the product or service has been developed, place a fair price on it. Your pricing can be adjusted during your market research, but it's good to start with a number before you hit the street. We are asking questions when we meet people so they will give us a good idea what our product or service is worth in short order.

With our product or service defined and priced, it's time to look outside and determine how many potential business relationships we have. What type of individual would be interested in your company's product or service? Are they engineers, homemakers, truck drivers, athletes, or accountants? Once again, we want to be specific and focused. Define your target customer in writing in just a few sentences. Remember, we can refine this description when we research our ideas with potential business relationships.

For example, let's say our new company sells business forms to accountants. We need to contact accountants with our great new business forms. How do we find them?

Circles

It's time for more circles!

Take a map of your local area including your city, county, and state. Draw a circle with your home or office in the center. The first circle should span one mile from your place of business. Draw several more circles expanding the distance out to fifty miles.

The most cost effective business relationships are usually the ones closest to you. The farther away you have to travel, or your customer has to drive to you, the odds of developing a strong working relationship diminish. Start with the circle closest to your place of business. Go to your local library and talk to one of the smartest people in the world, the reference librarian.

Building Relationships That Last A Lifetime

This wonderful person has a whole pile of reference books that will assist you in locating just about any business in the world. Many industries have trade associations (for instance, accountants) that publish their members' names, addresses, and specialties. Spend some serious research time at one or more of your local libraries. You will be amazed at what you can dig up with a little effort.

The Internet is of course another tremendous resource in locating potential business relationships. Search engines like Google, Ask.com, and Craigslist are all loaded with information on just about anything. If you do not have your own computer and Internet connection, your local library is a great place for free computer access.

As you search, remember we are looking for contacts within the bull's-eye. Too many times, young organizations jump on airplanes or drive long distances to secure their first big deal when their best shot at business was in the building next door!

Once you've searched thoroughly within the one-mile circle, move to the outer rings of your market research map. There are no magic numbers when it comes to a given market or product. Some organizations need thousands of potential business relationships to thrive. While others ventures need only a few hundred. A good rule of thumb is the ratio of ten to one.

This ratio is simple, ten qualified potentials to close one piece of business. The ratios for your business may be higher or lower, but this standard is a good one to start the research process. Keep in mind that this is only research and is always at best a guesstimate. So be prepared to rework your ideas early and often.

Suppose our library research has uncovered a list of accounting firms. The reference list contains the names of a thousand firms within fifty miles of our office. If we use the ratio of ten to one, we have the potential of doing business with a hundred customers. Can a hundred customers make enough profit for us to launch our new forms business?

If the answer is yes, get started. If the answer is no, does it make financial sense to expand the circle to a hundred miles? Perhaps we can expand our product or service offering so we can charge more money? Regardless of our tactics, we are dealing from a solid knowledge position, and knowledge is power.

Unfortunately, too many young organizations turn the lights on and start doing business without knowing their marketplace. This is a major reason why three out of five never make it through their second year in business. Simply put, some new businesses should never have been started in the first place, because their market did not exist or was too small to make a profit. Knowledge is not only power, it is tied directly to success.

Competition

Before you pull the trigger to launch your new company, you must spend some time looking for competition. Once you find them, you need to understand the "four Ws."

Who they are?

What is the price of their competing product or service?

Where they are located?

Why are they successful?

Once you have answered these questions, ask yourself, how will I separate my company from my competitors?

Asking and answering these questions are simple research steps anyone can do, but few get the answers early in the business development process, and then later they pay a high price for their mistakes.

If you plan on taking on some big competitors, you'd better have these answers written in stone before you start. If your product or service has no competition because it is so unique, then think about securing legal protection by obtaining a patent or copyright so no one can legally steal your idea.

Know your competition. They will quickly know you.

When the numbers look good, the people are committed, and the homework completed, it is time to start that new organization and reach out and touch someone. Review chapters 2 through 5 and develop your relationship-building process specific to your product or service. Apply what you know with the daily discipline of a seasoned athlete.

12.

Towers and Pyramids

Whether you own your own business or work for a large organization, understanding your personal and corporate relationship numbers is critical for success.

A successful relationship builder has a large number of contacts, prospects, and long-time clients that are all in constant development. For each one of them you will have a specific relationship campaign designed around their needs and future. As we discussed in previous chapters, the professional relationship builder is constantly "touching" and impacting the lives of their relationships as well as asking questions and making timely follow-up. Done properly, the client becomes more comfortable and trusting, and opportunities arise to do business beneficial to both parties.

Based on the skill of the relationship builder, the type of product or service offered, and the needs of the clients, a large pool of "prospects" must be maintained for high levels of success. This pool of relationships in process is a critical number of individuals and corporations and should be monitored very closely.

Relationship building that generates revenue (sales) is a numbers game. The more potential clients you have in the pipeline, the greater the chances of closing good business. If your goal is to earn a certain amount of money and you are paid on an incentive-based pay system (commission or pay for performance), then you need to "close" enough business to achieve your financial objectives. If you sell less, you earn less, and vice versa. With some simple math, it's easy to calculate how many prospects you need to generate a certain number of proposals or offers to close a certain amount of business and be paid an amount of commission equal to your financial goals.

Most successful relationship builders have a large pool of professional relationships they maintain. Just like our farmer, the larger the fields, the better chance of a larger harvest. How large is your relationship pool? If your business requires many successful transactions on a frequent basis, then your pool should be in the thousands. If your transactions are large and yearly in nature, your pool may be in the hundreds. The key to professional sales success starts with your pool. It can never be too large, but it is often too small.

The Tower: How Strong Is Your Business?

Picture a tall tower supported by nothing more than a very narrow foundation. Image what happens to this type of structure in a strong wind. Because the building is too tall and too narrow it will sway back and forth and give the occupants quite a ride. What would happen to the structure in a hurricane or tornado? The answer is disaster. The structure is just not a stable building, and anyone who trusts it will be disappointed or dead when the heavy storm arrives, and the heavy storms always do!

The tall tower with narrow base is like a relationship pool that has too few contacts in process. It never ceases to amaze me how individuals and organizations try to do big business with little numbers. The math does not work. If we want a long successful career as a relationship-building professional, we must have a large pool of prospects. The farmer cannot harvest thousands of bushels of corn if he plants only a few acres. Your field must be larger than the harvest you expect. Too many companies have too few prospects for their products or services.

During the growing years of our technical consulting company, our largest customer wanted even more help from our talented consultants. The client was one of the largest insurance companies in the world and was in the process of building a brand-new line of business. Cost was no object when it came to the computer systems vital to this new enterprise, and our company was the exclusive provider of technical talent. This was unusual since our firm was all of forty billable consultants at that time.

We were called to a meeting at the client's headquarters and presented with this fabulous chance to double our business with them. At the time, we had fifteen consultants working on the project. The insurance firm wanted to double that to thirty immediately and add another year of work to our contract.

What a fantastic opportunity for a young, growing firm! We turned it down. Why? By allowing this client to have 75 percent of our entire production, we placed our company in potential jeopardy. This opportunity would create a tower that could easily be toppled by a sudden downturn in the insurance business, a change of management at the top, or even a technology hiccup!

Even at fifteen consultants, we were too heavy with one client and one industry. As much as we wanted to take the business, we politely passed. As the months went by, we did add a few more consultants to the project, but only as we added new clients in different industries as well. We never wanted any one client or industry group to have more than twenty-five percent of our total revenue stream. By spreading out our entire production (billable consultants) across many different clients, we lessen the risk of any one client or industry having economic troubles and passing their troubles on to us.

As the company grew, we were always mindful of where our business was coming from and what industry segments we were working in so we could maintain the widest base possible. We never laid off a single employee even through two recessions. We avoided the mistake of the tower.

The Sears Corporation was famous (notorious) for buying the entire production of a company to serve their huge catalog and store business. Once the manufacturer was comfortable with the "good life" of working with one of the world's largest organizations, Sears would start asking for lower and lower prices and tougher delivery schedules. The manufacturer had little choice but to comply or lose their sole customer. The win-lose scenario was not the fault of Sears, but the manufacturer.

When we get lazy about building relationships for the future, we bring about our own problems. There is never one single relationship in business that will make our career, no matter how large or fabulous it is. We need many new and different success stories over the years if we are to weather the downtimes and flourish during the good ones.

Never tie your entire future to one industry or client. You may get your first big break from one player, but start adding new clients and industries as soon as possible. The clock is ticking before that next business hurricane arrives, and you want to be prepared for the big blow that is sure to come.

Look at your current relationship pool. Do you have a wide, diverse client potential, or is your company, and your future, sitting on top of a tower?

The Power of the Pyramid

The opposite structure to our tower analogy is the pyramid. By building our relationship pool wide and numerous, we create a strong and resilient base on which to build our business relationships and professional future.

Picture the pyramids of Egypt. They have survived one of the harshest environments on the planet for thousands of years . . . and they are still standing. The same will be true for your business if your relationship pool is larger and deeper than it needs to be. Your foundation can never be too deep or too wide if you are working each relationship.

In the technical consulting business, my experience taught me that our prospect database needed to have at least ten qualified prospect organizations for every billable consultant employed by our company. This ten to one ratio served us well.

Since we would always hire a quality technical consultant no matter what the client horizon looked like, our sales team needed to keep adding new prospects to the relationship circle to keep up. Seventy billable consultants required seven hundred in the relationship development pool. These numbers were minimums, so the more relationships we could maintain over and above, the better our results.

How many growing relationships do you need for your business? You need to know that minimum number and build staff, systems, and promotional activities to make sure it is strong and productive. On the other hand, if your pool has too many relationships not being worked properly, then you need either to look at your team's organizational skills and understand why the relationships are not being built or to hire a few more relationship builders. The fields must be large enough (prospects) and worked properly (salespeople) or your harvest will not keep the business healthy.

What ratios do you require to be a profitable enterprise? If you are unclear on these number, you probably have too few. Imagine a game of baseball where you were allowed five hundred strikes before you are called out by the umpire. Even a so-so hitter's odds would be pretty good. The more prospects, the greater your chances of success.

There is one danger in having too many prospects. The danger is not committing to building a relationship with every one of them. Having prospects that are not worked properly is like planting a field and never returning to work it. Your odds of success will be very low. Remember our straight line and circle? If we want a large prospect pool, we must be willing to make the touches to grow the relationships. When there are five hundred relationships, we need five hundred relationship campaigns based on the needs of each prospect. Anything less is a waste of time.

Senior managers and ownership can work valuable sales forecasts once the client ratios for their business and industry are understood. Some industry groups will require some study and analysis to come up with the size of the pool needed for success, but the effort is ultimately made worthwhile by giving the entire relationship team real numbers to accomplish when it comes to the everyday reality of building relationships. Remember, it's not about sales, it's about the quality and quantity of the relationships the enterprise supports. Sales are the end result of excellent relationship building.

Building a large, well-developed and maintained prospect relationship base is a strategic must for any company. Understanding how wide this base needs to be is critical to measuring the health of the business. Understanding the difference between a tower and a pyramid is a good start, but making the right choices in people, training, and systems will determine whether your organization is high and dry or very wet and wobbly when the next business storm hits.

13

Five Key Relationships to Build a Business

I built three companies from the ground up. I have the scars to prove it! Starting your own business requires building relationships in five key areas:

1. Employees
2. Outside advisors
3. Customer and clients
4. Family and friends
5. You

Employee Relationships

One of the key ingredients in any company is people. Talented, motivated, and properly directed, people make the difference in any business. Unless you are planning a small, one-person company, you will eventually need to hire some employees. This important step is were many new entrepreneurs stumble. Before you conduct your first interview for your very first employee, take a powerful step toward success: develop a well-defined job description.

Great Jobs Attract and Retain Great People

Too many people go to work every day without a clear idea exactly what they are supposed to do to be successful. Many have an overall understanding of what their department, division, or area is suppose to do as a whole, but few can point to a detailed job description that highlights five to ten measurable daily functions of their position.

As a new employer, you can start your business relationship with your employees on a positive basis by doing your homework. Take your personal journal and list several key duties that the person in your new position must do on a daily basis to be of value to your company. Once you have it completed, look at the list. Are these job functions important enough to pay someone to do them? If the answer is yes, you are ready to develop a career path for a future employee.

Lay out your future employee's day with tasks and duties. Now go one step further and bring in an education piece to the career path and take this position to the next level of value inside your company. Building a career path from a job description is powerful stuff. If we are looking for full-time people to become serious company assets, then we need to think farther than their initial duties. Mix in some training, outside education, and your own personal mentoring, and you can build a serious partner in success. Think about the first six months only, and you will end up with what you planned for: a six-month worker.

Building business relationships that last a lifetime is most important for your future staff. The words *empower* and *enable* are more than just buzz words to a new business owner who wants valuable employees. It all starts with a job description that grows into a career path. This important planning must be completed to a high level of *detail* before you start the search for the right person. You must have a clear idea what you want from the position before you interview. If you simply start interviewing and build the job description later, you will build the job to match the person. This is a big mistake. The person should fit the job and never the job the person.

As the owner of the company, you will make a list of what you think is important in this new position, void of any specific person. It's what the company needs, not what the person has to offer. By hiring to a position and not hiring to a person, we meet the needs of the company. When we hire to the person without a solid job description, we do not meet the needs of the company. We just like what we see in the person. This is dangerous to the organization, and unfair to the individual.

Don't we want good people? Of course, but they must be good for the company, and not just good! "Making room," "finding a spot," or "adding good skills to the team" are all catch phrases that mean someone did not do their company-needs homework first. When we develop a career path for a position and not a person, we have something exciting to offer. What does the position look like in six months? One year? And even five years? How does the employee get promoted? What is the next step when they are promoted? These are good questions that should have answers *before* the first interview.

Interviewing and Hiring Qualified Candidates

Once you have a good working career path for your well-defined position, you can interview people for that job. After getting to know an applicant during the first interview, invite the candidate back for a second interview and show them the career path. Ask the candidate if they feel comfortable handling the job duties outlined in the job description? This is a fair question, and the candidate has the information right in front of them to evaluate. Ask for their response in writing. That way you can see their communication and writing skills in one exercise. Take their written response and keep it in their personnel file along with the original job description.

Showing a job candidate a well-defined career path shows your professionalism and that of your company. Changing jobs is serious business. Why would someone want to work for you when you haven't even taken the time to think about what is needed in the new position they're applying for? If it's all in your head, how are your employees supposed to do their job unless they are mind readers? Defining a job description before interviewing, just like defining a project before starting it, makes personal and professional success possible and measurable.

I was fortunate to start my first company when I was very young, so I never really had much of a company structure that I had to follow as an employee. But I quickly learned how important it was as an employer to develop my positions carefully before I ever tried to hire someone. When we cut corners in building business relationships with employees we cheat them and ourselves. Turnover is a terrible thing in any business. Losing a good person for the wrong reason is usually the fault of poor management. That poor management can be traced back in most cases to a rotten, ill-defined career path.

When I consult with organizations that are having people problems, the first thing I ask for prior to any meetings is the entire team's career path. It is often no surprise that employee career paths either don't exist or are poorly written. When that's the situation, the first thing I do is spend time with management helping them get the troubled positions squared away. You'll notice I said *positions* and not *people*.

To get things turned around, you need to make sure the career path is correct and in line with the company's objectives and goals. Once you have that completed and approved, then you can address the troubled employee equipped with the right program. Very rarely is the problem the person. People are hired for the wrong position all the time. A poor hire can usually be traced to a poor job description and ambiguous career path.

Most of my early hires were friends. All we good people, but none of them had the sales skills needed be successful. The result of these poor hires was constant turnover, and tons of wasted time. Turnover can kill a new business, so we must take our time, develop a solid job description before we start talking to people, and hire to the job description. Any other approach will cost you time, money, and gray hair.

Hiring Family and Friends

Even with a good job description in hand, avoid hiring family members or friends. The reason why most family and friends make poor employees is your past relationship with them.

My family is my family. I've known them all my life. I accept the good and the bad without question. If I truly love them, then I'm always willing to forgive and understand when they don't act or perform the way they should.

My business relationships (including employees) are different types of relationships. The conversations, activities, and long-term objectives of these relationships are different from my family. There is a certain level of professionalism that surrounds a business/employer relationship that would seem uncomfortable in a family relationship setting.

When we have different relationships with the same person, things can get confusing. Do we fire our brother even if his performance warrants it? How can we tell our cousin that she has screwed up her last account? What will your aunt say at Thanksgiving dinner? Make no mistake, there are many family businesses that run well, and have for many generations, but they are the exception, and not the rule.

My general rule is no family or friends when it comes to business. As I've learned, things just get too messy when performance or family matters get mixed in with the company. Your children will always be your children; they may not always be your lifelong employees.

If you have family or friends working for you, be careful not to mix the wrong relationship building steps with the wrong relationship type. There are family touches that are very different than business touches. To protect yourself from lawsuits, poor morale, and nasty Thanksgiving dinners, you must understand the difference and stay on your toes to avoid costly conflicts.

Employee Relationship Circle

A relationship circle is just as important for our new employee as it is for our outside business relationships. They need to be touched on a regular basis too! Whether it's a note, conversation, meeting, or a reward lunch, everyone needs positive feedback (touch) from their managers and superiors. Great managers understand that and take time to do it, and keep track of it.

Studies show the number one reason why people change jobs is recognition and not money. My daily sales contests confirmed this point. We would all participate in a daily production contest with the winner receiving twenty bucks. Most of these sales professionals earned over $50,000 per year, yet they worked feverishly for $20! It was a big deal to win and be recognized. The twenty dollars was just a trophy. The recognition by the boss and your piers was everything.

Everyone loves to be recognized. Unfortunately, too many misguided managers recognize people only when they screw up. There is no better way to kill productivity and create turnover than by recognizing only failure and never success.

Even a failure, handled the right way, can be a tremendous learning experience for the individual and the entire department. Exploring what went wrong as a team, and using the failure as an example to learn from can sometimes be better for morale and education than a big win. It all rests with the manager. Do we really care about a battle, or are we interested in winning the war?

Incentive-Based Pay

People do work for money. Sure, they stay for recognition, but they work for cash! Trying to pay people what they are worth is a tough task and potentially dangerous to relationship. No one wants to be underpaid, and most people would view it a serious insult if they thought they were. The other side of the pay question rests with the employer. You can't pay everyone a million dollars a year, so what is fair? The answer for both employer and employee is incentive-based pay (IBP).

When you pay people on incentive, you pay for results. People who produce small results receive small pay. Larger results yield larger paychecks. The system is a dream program that takes a little work up front, and regular adjustments every six months, but the results are self-managed people.

Any position can be set up for incentive base pay. Take a receptionist position and ask yourself the following questions:

1. What are the baseline responsibilities and duties for this job?
   (Make a list of ten tasks.)
2. How can each of these duties be measured on a weekly, monthly, and yearly scale?
3. How much are these duties worth to the company if done well?
4. How much does a similar position pay in my area?
   (Back to your reference librarian and various online tools such as Salary.com.)

Take your list and value equations and prepare a compensation program. Start with a base pay structure by the hour or salary. This base compensation should be no more than 70 percent of the total package, which works well for most positions. Sales and senior managers may have their base be only 50 percent or less, but 70 percent is a good rule of thumb for everyone else.

If you feel your receptionist should make $25,000 per year, then $17,500 should be paid in a base package for a forty-hour workweek. The remaining pay package should be weighted based on the minimum completion of the ten job functions outlined. If the receptionist performs 100 percent on the ten functions, then they would receive 100 percent of their bonus.

When the receptionist exceeds the minimum measurement, a bonus program should go above the base program. There is nothing wrong with the position paying $27,000 per year for excellent work. Try to pay the bonus as often as possible even if the sum is only a hundred dollars. The more bonuses paid, the more recognition the person receives. Make a big deal out of every bonus. Remember, we all like to be recognized.

If a position is compensated for performance, then the performance criteria must have a scale that can be measured. If a job requirement can't be measured, then it can't be used.

Here are a few good examples for our receptionist position:

Building Relationships That Last A Lifetime

- The receptionist position is critical to the start-up of the office each business day, so the receptionist must be in the office before 8:00 to start-up all office systems prior to the office opening. These systems include, telephone, coffee, computer, copier, daily journals and papers, and any other functions deemed necessary. This task will be measured by prompt attendance, availability of all systems, and the general professionalism of the office at the start of the day.
- The receptionist will answer all incoming telephone calls within three rings. This promptness insures a high level of professionalism to our incoming inquirers and guests.
- The receptionist will insure all outgoing and incoming mail is sent and distributed by no later than 12:00 each business day. The receptionist will also make sure all mail supplies are kept current and ready for use.

Each of these job requirements can receive a rating on a scale of 1 to 5. The position can be rated by one or two senior staff members who spend time in the office and are naturals to rate these activities. Whether it is an office manager or the owner, little time is required to rate performance if performance is deemed important.

What if the receptionist fails to make minimum results? There is nothing wrong with paying them a less for the period in question and encourage them to improve in the substandard areas. If the individual continues to miss the bonus performance, make sure the standards are fair and reasonable. If they are, invest some training and coaching time with the individual. This will usually get them back on track.

Most people want to do a good job, so make their job description as clear and measurable as possible so you can hand out bonuses on a regular basis. With the right systems, people will amaze you. When the company has a good quarter, which employees benefit financially? The correct answer is everyone. Some bonuses are $100 and some are $10,000, but everyone on the team should share in the victory. We share in victories, so we can pull together in tough times. When only a few win, only a few will care.

Creative organizations take a small portion of everyone's bonus and tie it to the overall success of the company. This program further promotes team, and its teams who win. Set company goals and reward company achievement as part of an individual's overall incentive-based pay package. We want our people to achieve as individuals as well as teams, so our plans should reflect that.

Turnover

Turnover costs businesses huge amounts of dollars, morale, and lost relationships at all levels. Here's how to keep turnover a rare event in your company.

First, make sure everyone in your company has a good job description with measurable criteria tied to compensation. Achieving success in one's position depends on the employer first defining what success looks like in an employee's work.

Second, insure that every person gets a real performance and compensation review at least once a year without fail—no exceptions. These reviews are done in writing and in person by superiors and team members for the sole purpose of positive improvement. Good managers and supervisors aren't doing their job unless they are giving feedback to their team members on a regular basis, not just once a year. A poor review may reflect poor management more than poor performance.

Third, watch out for isolation. Every employee should have two or three others who keep a positive eye on them. People want to belong, they want to count. Organizations that understand this basic need of human nature to belong have little turnover.

Last, but not least, make a big deal about individual achievement. Everyone loves a compliment, and recognition from their peers, so make it a regular part of your operation.

Finding good people, paying them fairly, training them on new things, and keeping them happy over a period of time is tough work. No matter how creative, selective, and successful your organization is, you will have trouble now and then with employees. It's just the nature of the beast.

Write down everything and anything about your people on a regular basis. An employee's file should grow big and thick, full of written reviews, updated job descriptions, training plans, letters of commendation, and even a few corrective measures. When it's time for the yearly review, simply open the file. Everything you need to know should be there.

Make time for incentive-based pay programs with your people. It's worth any and all efforts you invest by creating loyal team members willing to do what it takes for the organization's success.

Building Relationships That Last A Lifetime

Ongoing Education

People cannot stay the same. They are either improving or decaying. As employers we must keep them improving for the good of our company and for the good of the individual. Company-sponsored education is a true win-win. The firm gets a smarter employee, and the employee gets valuable training. Every position in your company from janitor to CEO should have a training component built in.

At BALR Corporation, each technical consultant had a learning program they needed to complete to get their highest raise and bonus. Skills can never be maintained—they must improve, or you must retire. The marketplace is changing so quickly that the skills we rely on today will be of little or no value tomorrow.

Employees = Business Relationships

As the owner of your own business, relationships with your employees are very important to the success of your company. Working with people eight hours a day, five days a week builds many types of feelings and emotions. The goal in any employer-employee commitment is a solid business relationship.

Business relationships require a certain level of behavior and respect to work. Crossing these lines can cause problems for the unsuspecting employer. Problems like sexual harassment, wrongful termination, misplaced favoritism, and even civil rights abuses all occur when business relationships are not maintained, and working relationships become something they were not meant to be.

When you are working, your organization must maintain a professional level of relationship for your operation to run properly. Replacing business relationships with personal relationships in the workplace can be dangerous to both individuals and entire organizations. Although every company is unique, here are a few suggestions to keep things in a business relationship context.

Socializing Inside and Outside the Office

There is nothing wrong with enjoying the people you work with, but these relationships cannot become the center of attention in a place of business. When business relationships become personal, the rules governing the relationship change.

Personal relationships are relationships of equals. There is no boss or leader in a personal relationship. Unlike a personal relationship, a business relationship needs a hierarchy for things to run efficiently. When you introduce a personal relationship into a work situation, trouble is right around the corner because the employer-employee relationships no longer apply.

Emotions are the bedrock of personal relationships. Performance is the foundation for an employer-employee business relationship. The two foundations rarely mix well. Too much socializing around the workplace can cause problems if business relationships become personal relationships.

There is nothing wrong with a company picnic, Christmas party, or the occasional golf outing, but socializing two or three nights a week, or on the weekends, usually ends in disaster. Never confuse team building with friendship building. The two are very different.

Professional Respect

Everyone in your company should be treated with respect. Your company is a professional organization, and everyone who works in your company is a professional worthy of respect. From the way you dress, to the way you handle yourself in the office, everyone should maintain the highest level of professionalism, and expect that professionalism from everyone else.

Daily office activities can never be too formal. The problem occurs when activities become too casual. Your company will perform only to the level your team believes it can. If the team is sloppy, poorly organized, and undisciplined, the results will be similar. If the team is crisp, organized, and disciplined, the results will likewise follow in kind. Which results do you prefer?

Set reasonable and professional standards for conduct in your company. These standards make your company a great place to work. They protect everyone, and encourage all to succeed as part of a professional team. Good people are too valuable to lose. Build a great organization with good people and solid company standards that promote professionalism.

Lead by Example

As an owner, you set the tone for business relationships with your employees. If your conduct, comments, and work habits are less than professional, you have set a low bar for those who work for you. Hold yourself accountable. Your employees will take their lead from what the boss is doing. Consider the following questions and answer them for yourself:

How do you talk to people?

What time do you show up or leave each day?

How do you treat people?

How do you treat vendors?

How do you handle clients?

It would be interesting if you could learn what your employees would say in answer to these questions. Do you think their answers correspond to yours? If not, that's cause for concern and requires some serious soul-searching on your part. You cannot expect your people to go any farther than the boss. As the leader of the company, your example is critical.

Business is business, and personal is personal. When these two relationships cross paths in the workplace, bad things can happen. Be on the lookout for these scenarios in your workplace, and keep it professional. You, your team, and your entire organization will be glad you did.

Outside Advisor Relationships

Using outside advisors can help a new business avoid the painful and expensive learning curve. How to pay taxes, what contracts to sign, and how to handle cash flow are just a few business questions to be fielded by outside advisors. Trying to "learn as you go" can be very painful and very expensive. You will be well served by building long-lasting relationships with qualified outside advisors such as a good banker, a good accountant, and a good lawyer.

A Good Banker

Regardless of your cash position, your business needs a solid banking relationship. Just like finding your first clients, look for a bank as close to your operation as possible. Working with a financial institution that shares your neighborhood makes sense. Your clients are probably their clients.

Once you've identified three or four banks in the area, go see them. Meet the people who will work on your account. Have them answer similar questions about rates, fees, and services. Remember, that all banking services and fees are negotiable. Compare services and various banking products that you may need down the road.

When it's all said and done, the bottom line in selecting a financial institution is people. You will need a strong relationship with your bank and the people who service your account, so choose wisely. Make sure the banking officers are willing to invest their time into the relationship as well. Relationships require both parties commitment to succeed.

Talk with your bank about sharing leads with each other. You need new customers and so does your bank. Developing a solid business relationship of trust and respect can be good for both organizations. Start a relationship circle campaign with your personal banker immediately. This is a person who you need to have a strong relationship with, so a regular touch campaign based on a relationship circle is very important.

My first business banking relationship was very interesting. I was forced to start my first company out of necessity. The firm I was working for was a cooperative of several headhunters administered by a guy I will never forget.

Jim was a salesman's salesman. This guy could sell anything to anybody, and he did—from his drive in franchises to running a search firm (he never was a headhunter, but talked some of the area's best guys into his co-op).

Jim was a little loose with the co-op's money, and ended up putting the entire organization into financial turmoil. As we were getting ready to close the doors and go our separate ways, I closed a deal with one of my best clients in the insurance business. The fee for this placement was $10,000. The co-op arrangement called for the house to get 25 percent of the fee, and the recruiter to pocket the rest. The 25 percent was used to pay the phone bill, small office staff, and the rent. None of which Jim had been doing for over six months! After a little soul searching, I sat down with Jim and signed over the check.

Well you can guess how it ended: Jim took the $10,000 and wrote me a worthless check for $7,500. That bad check was the first deposit in my new company. On-Line Concepts Inc. was located in a basement with one small window above my head to be used in case of a building fire. The rent was $150 per month. With a two-line phone, small copier, smaller fax machine, and a desk that came in a box (some assembly required), I was ready to take on the world.

On Line Concepts was going to be a powerhouse in Chicago, but the first step was to open a bank account for all those fees that were sure to come.

There was as local bank across the street from my new world headquarters. The Bank of Wheaton was about to land the banking business of On-Line Concepts Inc. I called the bank and made an appointment with their business banking department. When I arrived I met the vice president of commercial banking, Mr. Michael Kinsella.

Mr. Kinsella outlined the many services of the bank, and how they could help my business grow. In a matter of an hour, we had all the proper papers signed, and I handed him my first deposit for $7,500 to open my new commercial checking account. Armed with my new corporate checkbook, I wrote two checks my first day in business. My first check was made to my new landlord, and the second draft to the telephone company.

The first full day on the job was exciting. I was calling everyone from family and friends to every client, neighbor, newspaper, or office supply company that would answer the phone. I set up my new answering system using my best radio voice and was getting everything in its place.

One of my first incoming phone calls was from my new banker, Mike Kinsella. I thought he was calling to schedule lunch and talk over the high-stakes world of finance. His call is still fresh in my memory after all these years.

"Mr. Rice, this is Mike Kinsella at the bank. Did you write any checks on your new corporate account?"

I thought that was a rather odd question. "Yes, Mike, I wrote two checks so far and was planning on writing another one later today for a copy machine."

The next words I heard on the phone still hit me right in the stomach. "Mr. Rice, your deposit of $7,500 bounced. You do not have any money with us."

That no-good con man took my client's fee of $10,000 and wrote me a bad check for $7,500. I was broke in my second day of operation! Mike asked me if I could come in and deposit funds to cover the checks I had written. I told him I would come right over and make another deposit.

When I called home and told my wife what had happened to her new "big shot" husband, she took it in stride like she always did and asked me what I was going to do. We had a little money in the household checking account. I needed $250 to cover the two checks, so I wrote a personal check as my first "good" deposit into my new company. This was going to be a very thin month in the Rice household.

My next step was to call my father-in-law and tell him the bad news. He was very understanding and wanted me to find the no-good so-and-so and run him over with my car and take his battered body to his own personal bank and get my money. We both agreed this strategy would not work, but getting a lawyer was the best course of action.

Before we ended the call, Dad gave me a little pep talk and asked me if we needed a short-term loan. I told him to hold that thought and see if I could dig myself out of the hole I dug. He chuckled and wished me well.

I called the bank and explained the situation, and laid out my plan. The bank could not offer me much in the way of a loan without collateral, but they did offer to hold any check that did not clear instead of bouncing them. I will never forget how this little local bank stood behind me during my rough start as a business owner. A good banker and bank is worth its weight in gold.

The end of the story had a silver lining. Not only did I collect the bounced check in a lawsuit a year later, I was able to make a quick deal with one of my best clients and collect an $8,000 placement fee in just three weeks, so the loan from Pops was not needed.

My first client normally paid placement fees in sixty days, but I explained what had happened and offered them a discount if we could get the job done and they could pay me in two weeks. Since I had a great relationship with their staff, they made an exception, and On-Line Concepts was saved.

I still have a copy of that first check in my office as a reminder of that valuable lesson. The Bank of Wheaton got acquired a few years later, and Mike ended up somewhere else. Unfortunately, I lost track of him.

Mike, if you're reading this book, thanks. I'll never forget your kindness.

A Good Accountant

Unless you are professionally trained in accounting, you will need an accountant as one of your outside advisors. The accounting and tax laws in this country are incredibly complex. Uncle Sam does not care whether you know the tax law or not. If your return is not done correctly, you will pay for it. So take time to select a good firm for this important task.

Choosing an accountant is similar to selecting a banker. Review their qualifications and get three or more firms to bid for your account. Establish fees and other charges up front and schedule regular check-up meetings to make sure your finances are in order.

Once you select a firm, you should have a detailed meeting every quarter and go over all the numbers. Too many firms do not know their *true* financial position, and make decisions based on best guesses. A strong relationship with a good accountant will make this problem go away quickly.

Have the professionals complete all state and federal returns required for your area. Make sure they sign them with you. If you paid them, their signature should be on every form right next to yours.

A strong business relationship needs to be started and maintain with this important advisor. Regular meetings, touches, and conversations should be planned and scheduled.

A Good Lawyer

A good lawyer is another business contact every company should have. Find counsel that your team is comfortable with. Ask questions, and get a feel for how they do business. Understand fees and billable hours before any work is done. Watching a good lawyer work a business opportunity or problem is fascinating. Just like with taxes, the law can be a very complicated subject, so choose wisely.

Until your company grows quite large, you will need outside legal counsel. Writing agreements, contracts, or other binding commitments as part of your business requires a good business lawyer to review and develop sound procedures and documents. Once your legal documents are developed, you can use them over and over again in similar circumstances. There is no need to keep reinventing the wheel.

Think of legal documents your company will need. Make a list of them and discuss them with your potential lawyer during the interview. Your attorney may even save you some money by streamlining your contracts and agreements. Saving money by avoiding legal entanglements is the main reason for using outside experts like lawyers and accountants. Every penny spent should be equated to money saved.

As your experience grows, try to write everything you sign. If there is any doubt to the legal nature of your documents, run them by your attorney. Learn from your outside advice professionals as you work with them so your legal and accounting fees will also pay for your business education. Always take a position of ignorance and listen more than you speak. Take copious notes, and always deal in writing. Remember, two heads are better than one.

Be a smart dummy. Get a good group of outside advisors *before* you ever really need them, and build a solid business relationship that you can call on to make you look good.

RON RICE

Customer and Client Relationships

One of the five key relationships you will need to develop to be successful in you own business is customers and clients. These are the wonderful people who will buy your products or services, and you must be especially diligent to build relationships with them all. There is nothing better in business than a client or customer who buys your products and services over and over again. Repeat business is a sign that you are doing something right.

The more time invested in knowing your customers, the more successful your company will be. There is nothing more important than the customer. Understanding what their needs are today, tomorrow, and in the future will keep your products and services current and relative to the market. Custom products and services require even more diligence in client care since you build a business based on the constant change of your clientele.

What is the best way to find out why your customers are buying from you, and what they will buy in the future? Ask them! Most will be glad to tell you what they like and don't like about your company and your competition.

Everything you do in business should revolve around your customers. You products, pricing, look and feel, position, location, and service and support should all be based on what your customers are telling you. Ask them every chance you get. Too many small businesses fail because they are built on what the founder thought, and not what the customer wanted. Ego and pride are never profitable. Let your company look exactly like your customers tell you.

In the consulting business, we were constantly working at the client's offices. Our people would work side by side with the customer's staff, building business and engineering software systems that benefited the client's business.

During a new consultant's orientation, our company stressed the importance of becoming the client's consultant. That meant showing up precisely when the customer's team did. Eating your lunch, attending meetings, learning new material, submitting reports and time sheets, and preparing status reports just like the customer's own people did. If the consultant was doing their job, you could not tell the consultant from the full-time staff, and that was the point.

Serving the client is your number one objective. Anything else is secondary. Relationships are about listening and serving. Not telling and selling. Do you want to build a great business? Talk to enough customers about what they will buy, and build a company to provide it. *Bingo!* You win!

As a company, we never did computer technology for the sake of the technology. We worked in a certain technology because our customers used that technology. We were rarely innovators; it was far more profitable to be followers. Every time we met with a prospect or client, the questions were always asked about the technical direction of the company. "What computer systems do you see your firm using in the coming years?" was one of my favorites. As the customer talked, we took notes.

Get a hundred or so companies using the same technology, and needing the same type of technical people, and you have a nice client base to build a business. If the technology changes, and it always does, you change with it or die. Every technical consultant who ever worked for us had to constantly be learning new things. Whether it was a programming language, database, or some newfangled communication protocol, our people were always learning.

This constant education was good for both consultant and company. The consultants increased their skills (and salary), and we were able to win new clients at higher rates. This constant change kept our people sharp, and our clients coming back again and again.

We missed the ball when it came to computer technology only once. Steve Jobs (the founder of Apple Computer) started a new computer company called Next Computer Systems. This new computer and software was very impressive. From a technical perspective, everyone who saw it loved it. We did too and bought several of the expensive systems and sent a group of consultants to training. When your consultants are in training, they are not billing, so the lack of billable hours plus their salary and benefits makes training an expensive investment. We gladly made these investments on a regular basis based on the needs of our clients and staff.

Unfortunately, Next did not sell very many systems in the Chicago market. In fact, it sold two major clients in the entire Midwest. Instead of waiting for the market to accept the new computer systems, we jumped headlong into the technology so we would be the "pioneering" consulting firm in the area. We forgot that most of America's early "pioneers" did not make it. Our Next pioneering venture went the same way; so did our money we invested. Like most business lessons, that one was expensive. The customers must dictate your product or service. Not your opinion.

I love talking to new entrepreneurs about their organizations. I can usually spot a winner or loser within thirty minutes. Here's what I look for:

Who is the customer or client this new venture will serve?

How much time has the owner spent talking with potential customers, and what was there response to the new company?

How many customers are there in the circles of influence?

(See chapter 11.)

What is your relationship development program to win customers?

(The campaign; see chapter 9.)

How many customer relationships are being developed each day, week, and month?

Simple strategic questions that every business needs to answer every six months. Outstanding companies are always evaluating what they are doing right and wrong. This is what the business world recognizes as a commitment to continuous improvement. Industry leaders are known for this perpetual posture of being a learner.

When you poll your client base, do it in person. It's not only another touch, but the client is more likely to share even more information in person than simply filling out a questionnaire or talking to a telemarketer. The biggest fans and foes of an organization should work for the company. Be your own biggest fan and toughest critic. Be honest, and always evaluate everything in your business on a regular basis.

After you complete your regular in-house soul searching, ask your customers what you are doing right and how to make it better. Listen to what they tell you, and carefully make it your own.

Family and Friend Relationships

Starting a new company requires a ton of time. If you are not willing to dive into a new venture 125 percent, keep working for someone else.

Your family and friends need to buy into this plan as well. My wife of thirty years could share many stories about my great new ideas. She would listen quietly, ask a few questions, and be as supportive as she could. She was my anchor in the storms of starting and operating new organizations. Erin made a wonderful home for me and our three children. As I look back to those days, I realize how important she was in making my businesses successful. Her tremendous job of running our home allowed me to concentrate on the business. Without her, there was no way On-Line, Whittman-Hart, or BALR

Corporation could have ever grown to the level they did.

My father-in-law was a great mentor to me in my personal, professional, and retirement life. His advice and counsel saved me many times. What I loved the most about our conversations was his advice. Being from manufacturing, my father-in-law had a perspective on the service industries, staff, and client relationships that I appreciated. Although our organizations were very different, there were many business situations we shared in common, and dad always had time for me.

My own father gave me a legacy on what it took to be a good husband and a hard worker. My dad never spoke to hundreds, never made a million dollars, never built his own company, and never saw the wonders of the world, but I never saw him miss a day of work, and he would work side jobs on the weekend whenever possible to earn a little extra.

Being raised dirt poor, my dad did not have many options other than hard work. That work ethic gave me a chance for college, the opportunity to learn piano, and a wonderful home in the suburbs. All the things he never had. Even today, my father could not tell you in great detail what my organizations did to make money, but he is very proud of me, as I am of him.

All new business owners need anchors. Make sure your family is involved with your business plans, and they will be there to support you through the good and tough times. Battling the world of business and having trouble at home is a deadly combination. Stability and understanding at home is vital for a new business to succeed, so do not overlook its importance.

Business Anchors / Mentors

If you are thinking of starting a business, or you already have one, think about your human support systems. Who can you call and talk about a challenge? It may be a business relationship or it may be a personal one, or a combination of the two.

Developing a support network is one of the best things you can do for your company and yourself. No matter what your business, background, or ideology, you need to constantly have your thinking and ideas challenged by someone else. It can be a family member, friend, industry colleague, or even your pastor. This support person will tell you how it is . . . anytime . . . anyplace. These individuals hold us accountable. Some may even make us feel a little uncomfortable.

One of the most dangerous positions any individual can be in is to be isolated. We all have blind spots from time to time. Wise people get others' opinions before they cross a dangerous street in life. If you have a little experience (we all do) and are willing to share a little, then you qualify to mentor someone else. Mentoring takes time and commitment, so don't jump in the pool unless you are ready and willing to swim!

There is always time to get another opinion. Build those support relationships and keep them strong. They will save your bacon someday.

Time

There are two things in life you cannot replace once they are gone. One is time, and the other is your health. A balanced professional life is critical to the success of any new enterprise. Any smart entrepreneur must step back for two days a week and take a breath of fresh air. There are no exceptions to this rule. No matter how awesome, profitable, or needed your new business is you must not sacrifice yourself, family, or friends on the altar of greatness. Those who fall into this trap will eventually lose their balance and fail.

Family and friends are some of the most important relationships we will ever have, and there has never been a business or great idea worth losing one good friend. When it comes to our wives, husbands, and children, we must be honest about the risks we are taking and the time required when building a new business. Take your best time estimates and double them if this is your first new venture. Your family needs to know what adventure you are planning for them when it comes to time and your new venture.

In chapter 16 we will talk about organization and its relationship to time. If you are not an organized person, be careful starting your own business. Wasted time will kill a new venture very quickly, so if organization is not one of your strong suits, then take some study time and improve your skills before you launch your new company.

Your Relationship with You

Before you strike off on your new business, it's time for a little self-examination. You must be your own best friend and harshest critic when it comes to starting a business. Take a long look at your planning, motivation, and commitment to this new venture. What are your risks and costs balanced against your potential rewards?

Remember, when you look in the mirror every morning, the boss is staring back at you. You are responsible for the results of the enterprise.

Building Relationships That Last A Lifetime

Running your own show will be the second toughest thing you ever do in life. The first is being a good spouse and raising children—now that's the toughest thing you will ever do!

Spend as much time as possible with successful business owner or operators. Watch how they handle themselves and their business. Learn from their mistakes, ask questions, and never accept anything at face value.

Everything you really need to succeed in your own business you already have. It's just a matter of using and refining what you already know. Nothing will ever replace common sense, hard work, and honesty.

Goals and Milestones

Set some realistic time frames for your new business, and be hard on yourself in making them happen. If you are constantly missing your milestones, then something is wrong with your plan, business model, or both. Stop and find the problem and fix it. It may be the idea, the timing, or a hundred other things, but you need to take a step back and investigate. Don't just change the milestone or timetable without a sound business reason.

Always set goals and objectives for your business on a regular basis. Quarterly goals and objectives worked best for us, but any program will work. Make sure your goal program is easy to manage and even easier to understand for the entire company. Working together as a team is what real goal setting is all about. You work as a team, and you win as a team.

The Greatest Show on Earth

Running your own business can be a very rewarding proposition. It has great ups and a few devastating downs, but the journey is worth it for those who honestly evaluate the costs and make the sacrifice. Be diligent in building your key business relationships. The better your support team, the better your overall business.

The smartest businessperson is not the one who knows everything, but the one who knows the best people who do know everything. Plan your steps, get more information than you need, listen and write twice as much as you speak, and never take yourself too seriously! Remember, it still is just a job.

14.

Just for Salespeople

Never Take a No,
or Closing for Dummies

This chapter is dedicated to my readers who serve for a living by selling.

As I mentioned in previous chapters, everyone involved in the business of life must have solid sales skills to accomplish their life's work, so we all need a little sales training to make the world go round.

Everything has to be sold. Even life-changing inventions like the electric light, the farm reaper, and the steam engine had to be sold. Thomas Edison gave away his electric light to many people before he ever sold one. Cyrus McCormick's reaper was almost smashed to bits when he first demonstrated the device. There was a time when people actually thought their heart would stop beating if they traveled faster than thirty miles per hour on a train! Every great idea in history still needed to be sold.

So how do we get people to accept (buy) something from us? Turn back to chapter 6 and review the seven touches to build trust. People buy things from people they respect and trust. We cannot build trust without action. The most effective action is relationship building. If we have done our work and built a strong working relationship, asking someone to buy is easy. With no relationship it is impossible to sell anything worthwhile.

If you sell apples for a living and someone walks up to your stand and wants apples, you are not selling anything. You are simply providing apples as a service, and that's a wonderful thing to someone who wants apples. If the individual wants apples and you are selling oranges, some salesmanship will be required and a level of trust needs to be established, or nothing will happen. You can outline the benefits of oranges, the high nutritional value, the beautiful color, and ease of use, but your odds are about 50-50 of changing the apple buyer's mind. Why? Because the customer wants apples!

A better strategy in our little scenario would be to direct the apple customer to your friend who sells apples. Make sure they have a good map, your card, and the instructions to tell the apple guy that they were sent by you. Not only did you touch a future customer, you sent a referral to the apple guy, and hopefully he will send some orange buyers your way.

When you provided a service, even though you did not directly benefit, you are building something awesome for the future. You will not change people's minds or behavior with pressure, gimmicks, or smooth-talking closing tricks. Sure, you may sell them once, but the high-pressure experience will ruin your future business and referrals for life, and you will *never* sell them twice.

If our apple buyer went home with your oranges because you needed a sale, what do you think will happen when he gets home and thinks about what just happened? He will be embarrassed. Some smooth-talking fruit salesman sold him a bag of oranges instead of apples! He will not repeat that experience again.

Do you see how shortsighted this approach is? You not only lost that customer for life, but everyone he ever talks to about the experience also. You offended hundreds of potential customers to sell one lousy bag of oranges. Our disgruntled customer will tell everyone he ever meets about the jerk who sold him oranges when he wanted apples. That could be a ton of potential customers lost. You won the battle, but you lost the war.

Before we move to close a deal, we need to ask ourselves two simple questions:

1. Does the client know me and my product well enough to trust me?
   (Seven or more touches.)
2. Is the product or service I'm asking them to buy of real value to them? *(Trust.)*

138

If you answer yes to both, then move forward and ask for the sale. If the answer is no, or there is doubt, then spend some more time with the client and solidify your answers to a definite yes before proceeding.

No Matter What, Never Take a No!

When we hear a "no" to our offer to buy something, we must understand what is happening. First, the client is not saying no to us as a person, just our offer.

Second, the "no" response could be from a lack of trust. Even if we have touched the client a minimum of seven times prior, that does not mean we instantly have trust. Some customers may take fifty touches to build trust! That's just how it is with some people, and we need to know that and keep working to build the relationship if we really want this client.

Third, your offer may stink! That's right . . . stink! It's not what we have to sell, it's what the client wants to buy. Step back and ask the client why they did not buy. When they give you the information, write it down and thank them. Once you have the information, either change the offer or change the client. You at least have the real facts and not raw emotion for your success or failure.

Always leave your emotions and ego at the door. This is a tough thing to do for type A personalities, but it clouds your judgment if you don't. Believe it or not, not everyone wants what you have to sell. Regardless of which problem you temporally have, *never take a no*. Instead, take a *not yet*.

When you get a hard "no," simply apologize. That's right, I would apologize. I made a mistake. I'm sorry for offending you. Your mistake was misunderstanding what the client wanted. Whether it was my service, product, or price, it was rejected. No problem, that is a "not yet" response. It may take years of "not yet" responses on some of your largest projects to finally get a "yes" response, but isn't a million dollar deal worth it? If your client understands that you are interested in building a relationship with them that lasts a lifetime, there will be many "not yet" situations between you.

If someone really means "no," then you have some fence mending to do. You have offended your relationship and need to apologize. No one likes to be pressured, tricked, or manipulated. A strong "no" response is usually a sign of a relationship mistake. Make a big deal out of a strong "no." If you want this relationship to last a long time, why lose it over one deal?

Going back to our farming analogy, the farmer picks one ear of corn every day before harvest to make sure everything is right before he breaks out the big machinery. He just doesn't start without carefully checking the crop first.

The same is true in closing a sale. You should be constantly checking the relationship for trust and to make sure the offer is right for your client. Then you can break out the big machinery and ask for a sale. If you are in a rush because of a sales quota, deadline, or just plain starvation, you will always get a no, and you deserve one! The corn is not ready for harvest!

If you're lucky and get a strong-arm sale, forget about that client for the future unless you are ready to apologize and start from scratch on building a relationship. Any relationship can be fixed with a ton of time and tender loving care, but it is difficult stuff. It starts with a sincere apology.

As your experience grows, you will know when to close just like a seasoned farmer. Talk with your clients throughout the relationship circle about the "not yet" policy of doing business. Once both sides understand that your relationship is long-term, then "not yets" will happen on a regular basis. Use the "not yet" experiences to build more understanding and trust with your relationships, and you will close more business more often then you ever thought possible.

There will be clients with whom you invest a lot of time and effort to build relationship and nothing profitable ever happens. Eventually you move these prospects to semiannual touch systems until signs of life return to that field. Make sure it is the prospect's actions and not your own that is causing the lack of success. It's also important to realize that there are some contacts who will never become professional relationships, and we need to identify them as soon as possible and move on.

Closing is a natural process just like harvesting. Perform your relationship development work correctly, and closing will become comfortable and natural. Should a closing situation seem uncomfortable or forced, step back and review your steps to date. Make the necessary touch adjustments, and move forward. Being uncomfortable on either side of the relationship is a warning sign. Watch for it, and take a step back. Relationships are marathon events. There is a long road ahead of any serious relationship builder, so don't push a relationship into an early death.

Referrals

Referrals are a good sign your relationship with a client or prospect is in healthy condition. Many sales trainers teach their students to ask for referrals every time you meet with a client or prospect. Asking the client or prospect for a referral is *not* a touch, it's a close. We do not close until we have developed trust. Asking for a referral prior to trust is dangerous.

Referrals are important to sales professionals, and we need to ask for them. Just make sure we do not ask until we have earned a client's trust. Asking a client or customer to buy something from us is the ultimate in our relationship campaign. If we've done our work in building a relationship, the field should be ripe. Some relationships take longer to mature, so make sure the trust is there before asking for an order or referral. Don't be disappointed if the answer is "not yet." It's just a matter of time and touch before it turns to a "yes."

15.

Harvesting

Sequoias or Soybeans?

Now that we have established the "yes" or "not yet" principal, it's time to understand what it means to harvest. When professional relationship developers have earned the trust of their contacts, asking them for something does not have to be a traumatic experience. After many touches, question-and-answer sessions, and numerous follow-up contacts, it is appropriate to close a transaction.

What type of harvest do you have growing in your field? Are you growing soybeans, which can be planted and harvested two or three times a year, or are you growing large trees like sequoias that can only be harvested once in a lifetime? Knowing what type of relationship you are developing is very important. Harvest too early and you waste the full potential of your relationship work. Harvest too late, and the crop may rot in the field.

Certain products and services such as life insurance are tree harvests. The real value is spread out over a customer's life, the life of their spouse, and even the lives of their children. If your business is selling clothing, your harvest schedule maybe as often as once a month much like a farmer who raises truck-farm crops like tomatoes.

Regardless of whether you cut trees, harvest soybeans, or pick tomatoes, there comes a time of closing a transaction and then starting the process again. Yet I'm amazed how many large ticket items I've purchased over the years and never purchased the same type of item from the same salesperson. I've owned at least twenty different cars and never bought more than one from the same dealer except once, and that was by accident and not from the same salesperson. Why is my situation the norm and not the exception? Most car dealers will tell me that it's two factors: turnover, and follow-up.

Remember when we discussed profiles and databases back in chapter 8? The database is one of the dealership's most prized assets and should be monitored and maintained. The same is true for any company database of contacts and clients. Regardless of who is making the touches, the relationship process must continue with as little interruption as possible. If the primary relationship professional leaves the company, his relationship development activities should be assigned to another team member as quickly as possible. The new developer contacts the relationships, explains what happened to ole Bill, and picks up where Bill left off.

Unfortunately, this rarely happens in most high-volume organizations, and all the relationship work and expense goes right out the window along with the future business. The relationship development process is the ultimate responsibility of the company that benefits from the relationship turning into a paying client. The company hires, trains, and compensates professionals to do the daily development work, but the company owns the overall effort and result. Organizations that understand this powerful responsibility reap tremendous benefits from lifetime clients and their ongoing revenue stream.

The years it takes to grow a tree may require more than one farmer to work the field over the many years it takes for the tree to be ready for harvest, but the results are usually large and profitable. The same holds true for the frequent harvest relationships, Even if the farmer quits, there must be another farmer trained, ready, and motivated to step in if the soybean field is to remain productive.

Professional organizations that understand what they are growing when it comes to business relationships must build and maintain methods, work force, and management if they wish to profit from their efforts.

PART THREE

Seven Skills
That Will Change Lives

CBCR

16.

Skill 1: Organization

As a coach, mentor, cheerleader, boss, teacher and even the occasional executioner, I have worked with hundreds of people to improve their performance. The seven skills discussed in this and the six chapters that follow are shared by the best relationship builders in the world. These are seven skills that will change your life! The techniques are simple, direct, and loaded with common sense. Their very simplicity is why they are often ignored or poorly applied.

Be honest as you review these monsters of productivity. Life is full of opportunities to change things for the better. If you are still breathing, there's still time to make a positive change in the way you do things.

The Value of Organization

Poor organization is the number one reason great people fail to do great things. Building relationships that last a lifetime requires organization in everything we do. From our time to information to activities, the more organized we are the better our results. Without being organized, we waste time, and forget important tasks. Homework, practice time, deadlines, names, the place, the price, the penalty, and the payment all are missed once too often, and opportunities vanish. Organization is skill number one for a reason. It will quickly improve or ruin your life.

Have you ever met someone who has more than twenty-four hours in one day? Since we all get twenty-four hours a day, our organization skills will determine how much we accomplish during that day. If we are not organized, we waste time. Time cannot be saved, stored, or replaced, so when we waste it, it's gone forever. When we are organized we do not waste time. We use it.

The most basic and most powerful organization system is a simple list. The great American inventor and statesman Benjamin Franklin used lists to make key decisions. Ben would look at a decision and make two columns on a sheet of paper. On the left he would list reasons for a "yes" decision to the opportunity before him. On the right he would make another list of "no" reasons to the opportunity. The longer list would dictate the decision. This wasn't the only way one of the wisest men who ever lived made decisions, but it sure is a good start!

Writing things down on paper gets your brain working. The more ideas, questions, numbers, and simply doodles you write down, the better you reason. Today's wired generation will no doubt prefer keying their notes on various computer devices (see chapter 5). The searchability of those notes is a good reason to go mobile. But there's simpler technology available and it works very well even when you can't get online or the power goes out. A great place to write things down is a personal journal. A simple spiral-bound notebook that retails for a dollar can change your life.

The Spiral Notebook and the Power of Journaling

Use a single subject notebook with the spiral pages to start journaling. The key to a good journal is *never* removing or losing a page, so buy a notebook that makes tearing pages out a problem (no perforated sheets). We want to keep every thought, idea, phone number, or good doodle intact.

Start the journal by putting your name and start date on the cover. When the journal is full, put the end date on the cover and file the journal. This is your personal business journal. I have over ten years of journals filed in my study. Think about how powerful that filed information is. If you prefer to keep an e-journal of one kind or another, go for it! We all have our preferences. But the point is getting the info in one place and being able to readily access it. When you are in a slump for ideas, simply go back a few months or years in your journals. I promise you the ideas will start flowing again.

Each day, put the date on top and start writing. It can be a list of to-do items, important phone numbers, ideas, or simply a good drawing of your office chair. It does not matter what you write. The important fact is that you do write!

At the end of the day, turn the page to a fresh sheet, date the top with tomorrow's date, and make a list of things that need to get done tomorrow. Never end your day without making your list for tomorrow. There is nothing more powerful than starting your day with your to-do list ready to go. You are ready to make the most out of your most precious gift—another twenty-four hours!

Run into a roadblock of ideas or activities? Turn the journal back a few days or weeks and see what was on your mind last week. Bingo! There you find an item or two that did not get completed or may need to be reworked, and you're back in business.

Never leave your workplace without your journal. You can take notes, schedule appointments, or scratch down an idea anywhere, so be ready with your journal and pen. Some of my best ideas came in the middle of my drive home. Always pull over and stop the car before you start writing. Same goes for smartphones, tablets, and the like. The people's lives you saved will appreciate your efforts.

The personal journal is your own special material. It may be a bullet-point list or sentences and paragraphs—all collected information is good information. This is personal, powerful, and productive material, so keep those ideas and thoughts coming every day. As you become more comfortable with journaling, the better your organization will become. It will seem a little uncomfortable when you start journaling for the first time. That is normal. Do a page every day, and soon it will become second nature.

Tape or digital voice recorders and other such devices do not work as well as a substitute for a written journal. There is something about writing that uses the brain unlike other media. Keyboarding seems to engage our mind in a similar way. It may be slow at first until you get used to doing it, but a written journal will pay huge dividends if you make the investment.

If you are considering starting your own business, a journal is the first thing to buy and start. Title your first new business journal and put the start date on the cover. Every time you are thinking about the business, make an entry in the journal with the date and amount of time you spent "working" on your new company. Keep all your notes, phone numbers, ideas, formulas, and other trade secrets securely in the journal. Always remember to record the date and time of all your work.

When the day comes to start paying taxes on your profits, all of your documented planning work is tax deductible! That's right, all of your work to plan, organize, and set up your new company was a start-up investment, but only if you kept good, legal, and accurate documentation on your time. No records, no deductions.

My journal came to the rescue with one of my largest clients. We were reviewing several important parts of the project plan during our third and final meeting. The process had covered over three weeks and hundreds of details. During a critical part of the final meeting, the client made an error in one of the key project details. I quickly turned back six pages in my journal and found the correct information.

I politely asked the client to review my notes. He was so pleased that I caught this important data, that he asked me to give him the actual pages from my journal! I told him that I would never tear out pages from my journal, but if he would direct me to a copy machine, I'd be happy to make him a copy. Those copied pages went to the legal department along with all the project plan notes to be transformed into a legal project description and final contract. All thanks to my journal.

Two weeks after our company won the project, I was visiting with the client. To my amazement, a personal journal was sitting on the desk of every employee in this large office. Not only did the divisional manager like the personal journal idea, he had special notebooks printed with the organization's name, the individual's name, and the start/end dates of the journal. These babies were hardcover, professionally bound books. They were beautiful! To this day, this five-hundred-person division of a major Fortune 500 company uses a personal business journal.

The famous inventor Thomas Edison was a huge proponent of journaling. Even though he had only three months of formal education, Thomas Edison was a tremendous reader, always searching for new subjects and ideas. The inventor's mother homeschooled young Edison after a teacher deemed the future genius "addled" and too slow to ever learn to read.

Not only did Edison learn to read, he was granted over one thousand patents in his lifetime. In one stretch, he was granted a new patent every year for sixty-five consecutive years! An incredible accomplishment considering he never went to college, or even a formal high school.

Edison kept copious notes on everything he was thinking about or working on. In his later years, the inventor had a full-time clerk armed with a Royal typewriter to transcribe everything the inventor was thinking, so a single thought was never lost.

Your Personal Journal

Once the journal becomes part of your daily life, things will start to change. Starting your day with a list that you prepared the night before is powerful stuff. The first thing you review over a good cup of coffee is your journal list for today. You may change an item or two, or even add something that crossed your mind while you were brushing your teeth. Your mind is engaged and ready to start checking off the day's to-dos.

As listing becomes a daily habit, you will be amazed just how much you can accomplish. The reason for your newfound success lies right in front of you in the journal. Take your listing one step further, and you can start planning and organizing your goals for the week, month, year, and lifetime. From losing a few pounds, to completing your college education, put your long-term goals on the top of each page of your daily list. You see the goals every day, and you can organize your daily work to make your goal a reality.

Remember, we cannot rely on our memory alone to get the things done each day. There are just too many distractions to stay on target. As we lose focus, we lose time. When things get crazy, we can simply go back to our journal list, and get back on track.

Another great benefit of journaling is history. After you have a couple of months of journals completed and carefully filed away, you can always go back and review what you were doing three months ago. Many times this information will trigger ideas and new productive thoughts, and sometimes just bring a smile to your face.

Don't miss out on using a journal, making daily lists, and tracking your personal goals. The benefits and productivity will amaze you. We live in a busy world. There are so many demands on our time that it is easy to get lost in activities that are not really important. Journaling allows us to step back and review anytime day or night. A journal helps avoid the memory mistakes by writing down ideas, to-do lists, and important information before we forget them. I know firsthand how a personal journal can change both your personal and professional life because it changed mine.

There two big mistakes you can make when collecting information. The first is writing nothing at all and relying on your memory. The second is writing things down on something other than your journal. Using post-it notes, napkins, or loose paper is a terrible idea when it comes to data collection and retrieval. You will lose them, and the important relationship data they contained.

Get all paper off your desk other than your journal. This will eliminate the data destroyers. Use your journal for everything, and you will lose nothing. Legal pads, sticky notes, and other forms of paper must be thrown away. Do not use them. Writing important information on this type of paper is trouble in the making.

A large part of building relationships that last a lifetime is organization. Journaling is one of the key daily activities of a well-organized life regardless of what you do for a living. The journal will become a permanent record of your life both professionally and personally, so keep it close to you at all times. You will be amazed how powerful this simple organization technique will become with a little application and discipline, and it only costs one dollar, but is worth a million.

Your Pocket Calendaring Device

The second organizational tool that all top relationship builders carry is a pocket calendaring device. These little gems have been around for many years. You may know them as Day-Timers, Franklin planners, or other versions and brands. Simply put, they are calendars that are easily carried.

In the last ten years or so, we've seen the onslaught of small computer-based versions of calendaring devices. Personal digital assistants (PDAs) have flooded the market in recent years. After many years of using a Day-Timer, I purchased my first Palm PDA device ten years ago.

The electronic version was a little scary at first, but it was worth the effort because it synced with my personal computer database, and gave me an easy backup to all my scheduled dates and follow-up information. This made my profile system much more powerful than just a paper system alone. Today my PDA is also my cell phone—a smartphone.

Powerful mobile computers with larger screens such as the tablet make onscreen journaling more promising. Regardless of which system you use, the key is using it! If we accept the power of the relationship circle, then we must keep a good working calendaring system with us at all times. Every time we touch someone of interest, we should be scheduling our next encounter *before* we say good-bye. This is very difficult if we do not have a calendar with us that covers at least six months in advance.

Building Relationships That Last A Lifetime

There are few things more impressive than a person ready to schedule a follow-up right now. Studies show that we have a very limited amount of time to remember a future activity once it is set. Short-term memory experts say the average person has less than thirty minutes of memory before some detail is forgotten. Only thirty minutes from the time you say good-bye until you forgot whether it was Friday the 20th or the 27th? A pocket calendaring device can cover your less-than-perfect memory in a few short seconds.

If your company has a corporate calendaring computer system great, but you should always have your own pocket system that you *always* have with you. There is nothing worse than having to check your calendar back at the office and then get back to someone. Have it with you and ready. You may not get a second chance!

If your guest does not have their calendaring device with them, you can make the appointment and send them a reminder note (another touch). Use the pocket calendaring device right in front of your contact. It shows them just how important you considered the next meeting.

Just like our journals, the pocket calendaring device is a great application that requires daily discipline for success. The device does us no good if we leave it on our desk or at home in our sock draw. It must be with us all the time to be effective. You never know when life will throw a great new relationship into your path. Be prepared to take advantage, or will you fumble, forget, and forever regret. Time is a finite commodity, and your memory will always fail you right when you need it most.

Use your pocket calendaring device to plan your daily activities. Working hand in hand with your journal, your pocket calendaring device will quickly become indispensable.

There will be a temptation to combine your journal and PDA into one. Don't do it. Using a PDA for journaling is limiting. Why trade a full sheet of paper for a small touch screen? Even the tablet doesn't offer as much writing real estate. In any case, we want more information and not less. The smaller screen tempts us to take fewer notes and details. Less information equals less relationship.

Carry both, your journal, and your calendar everywhere you go. When your calendaring device is full (paper versions), don't throw them away. Just like your journals, they can become great history reviews or help generate new ideas during times of creativity draught. Save them all and file them where they can be retrieved when needed.

Both your journal and your calendaring device are great places to keep business deductions and expense items for reimbursement or tax preparation. Keeping good records can mean thousands of extra dollars in your pocket come tax time. Once again: no written records, no deductions.

Imagine showing up for work every day with a list of important things to do waiting for you. It's empowering. The daily discipline of a journal and a calendaring device makes this a reality. Plan your life and work the plan.

Your Contact Card

The last of the big three organizational devices is a contact card. Regardless of what you do or where you go in life, you need a card with your name and all relevant contact information. You give these cards to *everyone* you meet.

It does not matter what you do for a living. Everyone needs a contact card. If you want to give someone your telephone number, give them your card. Not only will the information be correct, it shows the receiver that you think they are important. Contact cards make a great first impression. Remember too, a card always counts as a touch in the relationship circle, so make the touch a good one.

A recent development in cards is adding your picture. Placing your mug shot on your card makes it more personal and allows your card to stand out. This photo touch will make the card twice as expensive, but it's worth the investment.

Even if you are not in a profession or business that requires cards, get one made up anyway. Opportunities are always out there to improve one's position in life. You must be ready when opportunity knocks. You are important. Never think for a moment that you are just a lowly somebody not worthy of respect. If your employer does not provide everyone in the organization a business card, spend fifty dollars and get your own. Your local print shop can take care of the job in a few days.

If you own or run a company, let me take a moment and share with you one of the most inexpensive, guaranteed-results, empowerment tools ever invented . . . the business card. Every single employee in your company should have their own business card, and it should be of the same style and quality as the president of your organization. Why? Because everyone should be a representative of your company! From the janitor to the chairman, every member of your company should have their own card and be taught how to use them.

Building Relationships That Last A Lifetime

I have conducted business card training for years. It's not very difficult, but very important. The training is basically how to be professionally polite using a business card. When you receive a business card from someone else, you always return the favor by sharing your card with them.

We have landed some serious new business thanks to one of our staff who was not officially a salesperson, and it all started with a card. That accountant also received a nice dinner on me as a "thank-you" for being ready for business with their card. People are empowered when they are treated as valuable team members. There is no better way to empower everyone than to give them their own business card. It's inexpensive power in a small package.

Retired seniors, stay-at-home moms, and even the unemployed need a contact card. There is no better way to start a new relationship than by giving someone your card. We build relationships our entire lives, so why would we ever stop needing a contact card?

Once you have a card, you must always carry them just like your journal and pocket calendar device. Give them out as often as you can. You can never hand out too many. If you were one of my unfortunate staff to be caught without your card, you had to buy me lunch. If I asked you for a card, and you gave me one, then lunch was on me. I'm proud to say that my team hit me up for a lot of lunches, and I was glad to pick up the tab. It was a fun way to remind them that our success as a company was everyone's responsibility.

The Big Three

When you leave your bedroom each day, the Big Three should be on your person as you walk out the door.

1. Your journal
2. Your calendar
3. Your cards

Just like the old credit card commercial, "Don't leave home without them."

Life is full of opportunities and interesting people. Unfortunately, we cannot rewind the day's events like a video to review what happened and catch up on what we missed. We have to take notes and information on opportunities shortly after they present themselves. We have such a short time to record things that happen to us, so we need the Big Three with us and ready for action, so we can schedule and secure that next great relationship.

Don't let poor organization be your number one reason why you miss opportunities. Take the time each day to use your journal, calendaring device, and your contact card to manage your life. Daily application and discipline will yield fantastic results if we take the time to do the powerful things every day.

Encourage others you meet to use these organizational tools to benefit their relationships. Building teams of professionals who share a common goal of excellence in organization creates an awesome winning experience.

17

Skill 2: Lifelong Learning

One of my biggest regrets in life was never finishing my college education. Too much partying and too little study made short work of my first attempt, and lack of cash quickly ended my second try.

I poke fun at my lack of a college education in my professional bio by listing a PhD in business from Hard Knocks University. Most of my adult education did come from the street. Many people consider it the best kind of education. Although I agree with them to a point, I think a college experience is a better first step. I regret my poor decisions when it came to college.

My parents were blue-collar, hardworking people from the coal fields of Pennsylvania. Both of my grandfathers were dead by their early sixties thanks to breathing coal dust. My grandfather Rice insisted that his two boys would never see the inside of a coal mine and sent my dad and his older brother to Detroit, and to a better life in the car plants.

Although my uncle got a few college classes under his belt, my father had little more that a high school education. My mother was raised on a farm down the road from my dad. She went to secretarial school and learned the art of shorthand. She followed my dad to Detroit a year later as a secretary for the Ford Motor Company (she worked there for forty-two years). As I mentioned in chapter 1, my dad had two goals when he left home. One was indoor plumbing, and the other was a swimming pool. He accomplished both and made a nice home in the suburbs for his family.

My younger sister and I both attended Lutheran schools all the way through high school. This was a large financial burden on my working parents, but there was never a question when it came to education. My parents were determined that both their kids would go to good schools and hopefully college. In addition to parochial schools, we also had piano lessons, dance class (tap dancing), gymnastics, and many other such learning experiences. I don't talk much about the tap dancing.

When it came time for college, both my sister and I were less than successful, but I thank God my parents gave me the chance to attend. It broke their hearts when I decided my fortunes were elsewhere.

One of the key tools to insuring a successful life is education that never ends. The world is constantly changing. It is amazing how much change has occurred in just the last twenty years. Computers, satellites, medicine, music, engineering, communications, and even basic nutrition have all changed dramatically. It is impossible to stay current with today's world without an ongoing education plan.

I feel so strongly about education that every person who has ever worked with me has had an education plan as part of their job description. Their performance review had an education component. From the top down, everyone had an education program.

In the computer consulting business it was critical to keep learning new technology. We would hire a young programmer, and within their first six months they would be learning a new technology. Not only did this ongoing training make us more money, it made the individual more valuable to the marketplace. This was a real win-win for everyone.

Ongoing education was also mandatory for administrative and sales staff. We encouraged each individual to build their own educational program. Whether it was college-based, seminars, or self-paced programs, we were always pushing education with our people.

Lifelong education is a lot like physical training. You must constantly work your body if you want to stay in shape. People are not born with great bodies. Proper diet (real food) and a lot of hours in the gym yield results. Stop the plan, and within a few short months your body will change. Education is the same way.

Everyone should be learning on a regular basis for their entire lives. Studies show that seniors who do cross word puzzles reduce the risk of

Alzheimer's disease. Young children show dramatic brain development thanks to their parents who read to them from an early age. The scientific journals are full of positive research in regard to lifelong learning being a worthy pursuit for all ages.

My personal library continues to grow with new volumes. Most of the writing time for this book was spent in my study facing a wall of books. I've read them all, and each has affected me. Reading did not come easy. It took time and a little incentive from one of my first mentors, my father-in-law, to get me started.

My $2,000 Television

Erin and I were trying to buy our first house. We had rented a nice ranch style home with the option to buy. As our lease was ending, we notified the owner that we would be purchasing the property. Unfortunately, we were $2,000 short of our down payment.

My father-in-law is a great influence in my life. A successful entrepreneur in his own right, he has always been one of my most trusted life advisors. It was natural for me to seek his advice (and his checkbook) in this situation.

As I spoke with him on the phone, I could tell he had a plan for us to purchase the property. That plan changed my life. Dad came up with this solution for the $2,000 by buying our television and video player. This was a great deal for us since our old nineteen-inch set was worth maybe $500 with the VCR.

The second part of the deal was a little more difficult. No television in the house for one year! We had three small children at the time who loved *Sesame Street,* not to mention my sports on ESPN! Face it, we loved our television.

That was the deal: A check for $2,000 if we agreed to keep television out of our home for one year. We took the check.

The first few months were tough. Actually, Erin and the kids did a much better job living without the boob tube than me. Thank God for tolerant neighbors who followed the Bears and Bulls. I was a regular visitor.

During my third month of television drought, I stumbled into my first bookstore and started thumbing through a few business books. One particular book caught my attention. The book was *Iaccoca*, his first autobiography. Being from Detroit, and having a mother who worked for Ford, I thought this book would be interesting, so I bought it. *Iacocca* was the first book I ever bought for my own enjoyment. Luckily for me, it was a good read and finished it in one night. Reading became part of my life for good.

The local book stores were packed with business biographies. Many were out of print and could be had for half price! As a new business owner, business biographies seemed a natural choice. Audio books and various training materials on tape were added to my library in later months. Awesome sales and time management training from the legends in the business turned my car into a rolling classroom. Spending thousands of hours in my car was turned into hundreds of hours of learning thanks to Nightingale Conant. This company offers a wide variety of recorded training materials, and I was one of their best customers.

Every one of my employees was encouraged to borrow books and tapes. I became such a zealot on this topic, I started buying and ordering two copies of everything. One for my library and one to give away! The idea of giving away books was another one of my father-in-law's favorite hobbies. He had shared many great books with me over the thirty-three years I've known him. Several were life-changers. Thanks, Dad.

The one year without television went by slowly, but productively. We did buy another television, and today we own several, but the love of books and reading is just as strong as ever.

Have you read any good books lately? There is no excuse not to get started reading. It is far more productive than television, and actually expands your vocabulary and brain function. Watching television is fine in moderation. But reading has so many benefits, we all need to spend more time doing it.

Focus on Your Communication Skills

Regardless of your current or future position in life, don't forget to build your communications skills as part of your lifelong learning campaign. The sharpest people I ever met in life had two things in common. First, they could write, and second they could speak. Having the ability to write and professionally deliver your ideas in a verbal presentation are two of the most powerful skills you can ever master.

People who can speak in public and write their ideas in logical sentences and paragraphs end up in the best career, social, and personal situations. The reason for this is obvious, they can share their ideas better than the average person, and therefore they are quickly elevated into a leadership position.

There is only one way to become a better writer or public speaker, and that way is practice. There are some excellent programs offered by organizations like Toastmasters that promote public speaking among their members. Check with your local college, chamber of commerce, or library for speaking clubs in your area, and join one. The better you speak, the larger the fortune you can seek!

Good writing skills can be taught, but the more you write, the better your writing will be. Few people start off enjoying writing. From penmanship classes to the good old term papers, most of us have bad memories when it comes to writing. Break out by forcing yourself to write instead of grabbing your phone. Just like reading, writing will take some time to get comfortable, but it's worth the effort.

I have a close family friend who unfortunately made some bad decisions and ended up in prison in his early twenties. Don is now in his thirties and spends much of his day reading, writing, and working on the occasional carpentry project of building homes inside his prison walls.

Since the only way I can communicate with Don is by letter, we write often. Don has little college education, but he is one of the best writers and well-rounded individuals I know. He became this way through reading and writing. Even though he has to write his letters longhand, they are perfectly laid out, spelled properly, and well organized. He can converse on many different topics from HVAC design and repair to the latest spy thriller. He could easily pass for a college-educated business executive simply with his written words.

There is no excuse not to master the basics of writing. High school graduates should be required to submit a final essay before they are granted a diploma. Sending kids into the job market without the basic skills of reading and writing is wrong and should not be allowed anywhere in this country.

Just like training to be a world-class runner, great writers write, write, and write some more. Start small with personal letters and e-mails, and work your way up to personal résumés, home project plans, and small projects at your church, club, or office. As your skills grow, look for more opportunities to hone your craft.

Forget making that telephone call now and then. Write a letter. It means more, and you will learn more as well. Plus, it's a nice touch and counts as one too! Who gets personal letters in the mail anymore?

For those of you still in high school or college, take your communication skills to an even higher plateau and learn another language. The world is quickly becoming one large neighborhood and marketplace. It is arrogant and shortsighted to assume everyone will speak and write in English. Want to double your future salary? Learn to speak and write in another language.

Pathways to Lifelong Learning

What are you doing about lifelong learning in your daily routine? Whether you have no formal education or several doctorates, ongoing education must be part of your life if you wish to enjoy a lifetime of strong relationships.

Interesting people are usually well-read. They simply have more things to talk about. They have more things to talk about because they are always learning something new. Here are some ideas to help you get on the lifelong learning path.

Read, Read, and Read Some More

People who read are smarter than people who do not read. That's a fact.

I was raised on television. I can sing you the theme song of every popular television show in the late '60s and '70s. I learned a lot about life from *The Munsters, The Addams Family, Lost in Space, The Flintstones, The Jetsons,* and the ever popular *Three Stooges.* Needless to say, I had a lot of catching up to do when it came to learning once I got started in my early twenties.

Parents, get your kids reading early and often. Set limits on those video games, movies, and television programs. Make reading a priority early, and you give your children the incredible gift of lifelong learning. Teach your children how to learn. Show them a library and the wonderful world that books offer to anyone willing to turn a page.

If you are not a regular reader, start with the newspapers and stay current with what's happening. Whether you use the Internet or the newsstand, you need to read a couple of papers a week to stay in touch with what's happening in your neighborhood, country, and the world.

The Company Library

Our business staff was required to read three newspapers per week as part of their job. Since our operations were in Chicago, our three weekly required reads were:

The Daily Journal (local)

Chicago Tribune (state and national)

The Wall Street Journal (business)

We also kept an active book and magazine library full of industry trade journals, technical manuals, and textbooks. We encouraged everyone to stay current with what was happening. Every company should have a well-stocked office library and encourage people to use it.

Reading local, state, national, and international news is a great way to keep learning. Every time we read, the brain is stimulated and active. Use it or lose it. You can get a lot of this information by watching television. Your favorite news show is nothing more than someone else reading the same material you can find in the newspaper, and the newspaper has more detail!

I enjoy a good movie mystery. The Tom Cruise legal thriller movie *The Firm* was one of my favorites. I finally read the book by John Grisham a few months ago. Wow, what a difference! The book was twice as exciting as the movie. The same is true of most movies. The book is always better.

If you were born after 1950, you grew up with television. Unfortunately, we have become to visual as a culture and need to see things to learn. The brain is an awesome creation, but television can sometimes limit our potential, so we need to read at least as much as we sit in front of the tube.

Your Personal Library

Books are the key to knowledge. I've never heard of a subject or topic that does not have at least a dozen books written about it. Under the title "relationships" there are hundreds.

Looking for a good book on a topic of interest? Your local library will have several. If not, they can find one for you! Libraries are the most underutilized and most unappreciated public blessings in this country. Even small towns have libraries. The major metro areas have libraries so large they call them resource centers. These awesome places are great places to spend some time, and they are free! Unfortunately, most people cannot tell you where their local library is located.

A library can open the entire world up to anyone with interest. An entire college education is accessible to anyone who can read and is willing to take the time. Visit your local library. Ask for a tour of the facility and learn how to use the many resources available, including e-books. Librarians are very helpful people and love to get people excited about their facility. Step up and ask, and you'll be amazed by the opportunity for lifelong learning located right down the block.

There are two good reasons for starting and maintaining your own personal library. First, you can easily grab an old favorite and enjoy it all over again from the comfort of your sofa. You never get all a book has to teach you in one read. Sometimes it takes many different reads to gather all the information from a good book. The greatest book ever written, the Bible, still amazes me with new insights every time I read it. Owning your own copy of a good book allows the material to give you knowledge over and over again.

The second reason for having your own personal library is sharing. I love to own two copies of a great book. Giving someone a good book opens up a whole new world for them. I cannot think of a better gift than a good book. They also make a great relationship-building touch.

When I give someone a book, I ask them to pass it on. If they were moved by the material, buy another one, and share it with someone else. Think about a world where everyone did this.

One of my favorite authors is Dr. James Dobson. Dr. Dobson is a clinical psychologist specializing in child development. He has written many books on raising children, nurturing families, and their relationships. His legacy is an organization called Focus on the Family, a ministry that continues to be one of the true champions for families in the world. I own several copies of each title written by Dr. Dobson. I love giving them away to young parents, grandparents, and anyone who is interested in family issues.

Keep books in your home. They are a great source of lifelong learning, and they are a great way to serve others by passing on the gift of knowledge.

Audio Training Programs

Cars are incredible inventions. They can take us anywhere in the country. Even if fuel prices were $10 per gallon (they've averaged between $3 and $4 per gallon in recent years), most people would still drive a car.

The average American spends 5 percent of their entire adult life in an automobile. Using a portion of our driving time to learn is a great idea, and it's so easy to do. I love listening to good music when I drive, but why not learn a thing or two as well. Mix it up. A little music, then a little learning and next thing you know you can speak a foreign language!

There are hundreds of learning programs on tape and CD. Your local library will have many great titles to check out. You can also get digital audio books on CD as well. Using your car as a rolling classroom is a great use of time and facilities. If you have to drive, why not learn?

Just like good books, good audio programs should be purchased and shared. The Internet offers a wide range of audio training programs, and there is something for every interest or topic. Audio training programs are also available for download online (more on that below). Share good links with others.

Owning audio training programs is a great idea for a company. Purchase audio programs that teach skills needed by the organization and make these programs available through your company library. People can simply check them out and listen and learn during their commute.

Seminars

I love a good seminar. Whether it's on investing in stocks, buying corporate debt, owning real estate, or collector cars, a good seminar is worth its weight in gold!

Depending on where you live, there is always a good seminar being held at your local community college, library, church, or civic center. Talk to your reference librarian or your local chamber of commerce. Many of these events are free of charge. Don't be afraid to plunk down a few dollars now and then to learn something new if there is a fee to attend. In many cases the cost is tax deductible if it is related to your job.

If you work in one of the professional disciplines like law, medicine, or engineering, ongoing education is required to keep your license, but that should be just the beginning of your ongoing educational experience. There are new skills and techniques being developed every day in every discipline. If you want to stay current in your field, then ongoing education must be part of your business.

Remember, the day you learn something new, it becomes yesterday's technology tomorrow!

The World Wide Web

The relatively new frontier of the Internet opens up huge opportunities for lifelong learning. Every topic imaginable can be found on the Internet, and a training program to go with it!

We could spend a hundred pages talking about the learning opportunities on the Internet. There are just so many great programs. Many of these self-paced learning programs are simply amazing. You can study everything online from auto repair to law. If you have an Internet connection, you can learn anything! If you don't have access to the Internet, your local library can provide it to you for free or at very little cost, so there is no excuse not to use this powerful medium for learning.

If you plan on living on this planet for another ten years or so, you need to get used to using a computer. Whether you love or hate them is immaterial; they are here to stay. Your local community college has tons of great evening classes on how to use a computer. There are hundreds of people just like you who can't turn the stupid box on, so you will not be alone.

A personal computer connected to the Internet opens up an entire new world of learning and communications. Everyone should have access to and knowledge about a networked personal computer. If you can't afford one, get to your local library and use one for free. The possibilities are endless. Don't let your age, background, or fear keep you from enjoying and experiencing one of the true wonders of our modern age. Get educated and get surfing!

Back to School

Going back to school is always a good option for lifelong learning. Regardless of age, previous education, or professional background, a good local college offers excellent programs for expanding our knowledge horizons. We need only pick up the phone and ask a few questions. The cost of a good community college is very reasonable, and you learn the same material as those attending Harvard! There's no reason not to attend.

Most companies offer some form of tuition reimbursement for their employees. Unfortunately, too few take advantage of this great company benefit.

Learn How to Learn

When interviewing computer programmers for our company, one of my favorite questions was, "How would you learn a new computer language or a new software package quickly?" This was an important question because our industry was adding new technology every six months, and we needed to have all of our programmers stay current with the latest languages and software. Many times, there was little or no formal classroom training available because the technology was brand new, so we needed to have our people be "self-taught" on many of these new features.

As a company, we would buy all of the new software and manuals we could and send them home with our programmers. The programmers would load up the new software and work with it until they felt comfortable using the technology on the job. For some of the major new software, we would buy a dozen or so copies so we could have multiple people learning at the same time. As you can see, hiring people who knew how to learn was very important to us as a computer consulting company, but it's also important for any company to hire people who know how to learn.

What about your current job and job skills? Are they current or older skills? One of the best ways to keep a job is to keep improving your skills. None of us can stay the same when it comes to job skills. We are either getting better and more valuable to our employer, or we are quickly passing away into unemployment land. The choice is ours.

If your company does not offer education or tuition assistance, pay for it yourself. There is no better financial investment you will ever make than education for you! Don't be fooled into complacency. The world is getting smarter and smarter; you need to do the same.

Lifelong learning helps us build relationships that last a lifetime. The more educated we are, the more people we can meet, understand, and build relationships with. Never learning anything new makes us dull and boring. Not only do we cheat ourselves out of the excitement of learning something new, we cheat our friends, family, and other relationships out of the opportunity for us to share new knowledge with them.

You've already taken a step to lifelong learning by reading this book. Great! What's next in your lifelong learning adventure? Think circles when it comes to learning. Once we start, we never stop.

18

Skill 3: A Positive Self-Image

What do you see when you look in the mirror? It depends, doesn't it?

Did you know that the body cannot achieve what the mind cannot see? Think about it . . . If you think you can, your body believes it. If you think you can't, the body believes that too. We are on the road to success or failure before we ever leave the house!

So are you a winner? Or are you a loser? How do you see yourself?

Everyone wants to be a winner, yet too many of us sell ourselves short right from the start. Depression, anxiety, paranoia, and a host of other mental illness are on the rise. What was considered crazy, obscene, and socially unacceptable views and actions are now commonplace on television, radio, and daily life on the streets in many of our large cities.

It is no wonder why many have a poor self-image. Today's society believes no one is good enough. There is no way we can take an interest in someone else if we think our own image, life, and accomplishments are a pile of trash. We are trapped in our distorted view and are rendered helpless by the deception. It's time to clear the air of this nonsense.

I believe in God, and my God *never* makes a poor product, and my God made you. You are a marvelous creature, unique and unlike anything else in the universe, and anyone or anything that tells you differently is crazy!

Ladies and gentlemen that is a fact. You are awesome, and you need to think that way! Sure you have warts—we all do. Mine are probably worst than yours. We have to stop beating ourselves up about what we've done or where we are. If we can't shake the bad stuff, it may go all the way back to our spiritual relationships, which we talked about in chapter 3. If we want a healthy identity and outlook, we cannot afford to neglect our most important relationships, not least of which is a spiritual relationship with God. Get things right with Him, and you'll have a way to deal with the negatives and believe the positives about you are true.

Life is a marathon, not a sprint. Unless you know today is your last day on earth, there is always time to make things better. You start with a positive image, and match that with a positive outlook on the day. One day at a time. Remember, we want to fill our mind with positive things so our body is charged up to do positive things. The negatives in our mind suck the life from our bodies, and leave us depressed and disappointed.

If you see yourself as a no good bum, your body will eventually accept this falsehood as fact and do it's best to become the vision of your misguided mind. If you see yourself as a winner, champion, leader, best friend, and overall great person, your body will follow that vision as well. The choice is yours. Let's choose the positive and live that way.

We all want people to think good things about us, but it is more important for us to think good things about ourselves. People can sense confidence or fear. Both start with a positive or negative self-image. The choice is ours.

WYSIWYG (What You See Is What You Get)

Pictures are a great way to keep positive images in our minds. The more the better. Place positive pictures next to your mirror. Every morning absorb the images about where you are going and how wonderful it will be when you get there. The body cannot achieve what the mind cannot see.

Every person who ever worked directly for me was taught the reality picture game as part of their professional training. The reality picture game works like this. Think about what you would like to have in your life if money were no object. Cars, boats, houses, jewelry, kids, dogs, or a baseball team—it did not matter. Once you determined what your grand prize would be, find a picture of the prize and place the picture of your treasure on the wall of your office, cubical, or some personal work space.

Every day take a look at the picture and see yourself enjoying the prize in your mind. What color will it be? How will it sound? What will it feel like when you are enjoying it with family and friends? These are all *positive* images you are running in your mind. Your body will respond with more energy and focus if this becomes part of your regular work routine.

I cannot tell you how many of these special prizes became reality, but I know many of them did. Why? Simple. The work ethic, discipline, goals, and daily hard work brought the dream into reality. The mind saw it as real, and the body simply complied!

The same positive picture should be part of your compensation. Talk to your manager about what you need to do to get a raise or promotion. Be specific and make a list of those job responsibilities you need to exceed to get that pay raise or promotion.

If you work for a company or individual who will not help you reach that next level, find another job! Life is too short to waste on a company or individual manager who is not interested in you reaching your maximum potential. It should be a manager's top priority to bring out the best in all their people.

Many of my closest employees where usually salespeople, and their compensation was always based on commission. Every performance review, we would talk about money. What was a large amount of money to them? What was their financial goal for next quarter? The reason why I encouraged all of my people to get specific about money was development of a positive image. I wanted them to see success in their own minds. My job was to help them exceed their vision.

Large sums of money cannot make people happy, but it sure doesn't make them that miserable if handled properly! Every one of my salespeople knew how much they needed to sell to make $1 million in a year. That's right . . . a million bucks! We would work the numbers, and based on their compensation plan, we knew the amount of production required to earn $1 million in take-home pay.

We never had a salesperson earn $1 million in one year, but we had several get pretty darn close. I was cheering for them the entire way, and their positive personal image lit up the room wherever they went. Anyone who met a person on a mission knew there was something different about them. That difference was a positive mental image.

What image does your team have? If you are the boss, it's part of your job to get it as positive as possible. The results will build your bottom line, and make your office a great place to work.

Your Résumé

Do you have a current résumé? The reason why you should keep an up-to-date résumé is positive self-image. When you start feeling a little down, pull out your résumé and review your accomplishments. This is also a good time to add any new victories to the text.

If your accomplishments are a little light, no problem. Put together a plan to add a skill or two, or maybe it's time to change jobs or careers. No one can stay the same. We are either getting better or getting worse. Your résumé tells you what you've done, and what you need to do.

My résumé is updated once a year even in retirement. Although there is not much new to add, it's a positive experience to make sure everything is current and up to date.

Résumé styles very widely, but one thing all good résumés have in common is length. Keep your résumé to one page if you are just getting started in your profession. As you gain experience, your résumé can grow a page or two, but keeping it brief and to the point is critical. Remember, you have a very short period of time to make a good impression once a person decides to read your résumé, so make your words count.

Having reviewed thousands of résumés during my career, I've seen some fantastic one-page masterpieces, and a few five-page disasters. The following page includes my résumé as an example. Hopefully it gives you some ideas to develop or improve your own.

The Professional Background of Ronald R. Rice Jr.

Personal

Married for 30 years to my high school sweetheart Erin. We have three children: Christine (29), Corie (27), and Kyle (24). We live on the water year round in one of two places based on the time of the year: Lake of the Ozarks, Missouri (summer) or Ft. Myers, Florida (winter).

Education

I left college after three months and returned only for the occasional business class or seminar. My education came from two sources: experience and self-study. Having started my first company at 22 and retiring at 42, my career has offered me many great experiences in building organizations and working with great people. My personal library contains hundreds of books and an extensive audio training collection. I continue to learn daily, and hope to continue my education program as long as I live.

Experience

Over the past twenty-five years it has been my privilege to be part of three organizations as a founding member. During this time, I've personally hired over 600 people in a wide variety of skills and professional disciplines, trying to learn something different from each one.

After graduating from high school, I spent two years working in radio as an on-air personality and advertising salesman. My wife and young daughter traveled the country with me in a motor home in my second sales position as a regional wholesale bicycle representative covering a territory of nineteen states.

In the early '80s, I began my professional consulting career as the founder/owner of an executive search firm specializing in recruiting technical developers. After growing the business to six full-time recruiters, I sold the firm to two of my senior staff members.

In the mid-'80s, I was fortunate to work as the first sales/recruiting executive for the technical consulting company, Whittman-Hart. As employee number 14, I spent four years with the company as head of sales and recruiting. With a great inner circle of outstanding people, we were able to grow the organization to over 500 consultants in three branch offices. Our IPO was one of the most successful in NASDAQ history.

In the late '80s, I left Whittman-Hart to start my third organization. Joining with my two founding partners, BALR Corporation became a highly regarded technical consulting firm serving business and engineering clients across the Chicagoland area. Starting with only 4 original consultants, we were able to grow the company to over 100 full-time technical professionals within our first ten years in business. During this time, we maintained a strict "no layoff" policy. This "employee first" model was uncommon in our industry, and we were regarded as one the top organizations in our market by both our competitors and employees.

In 1999, I was able to negotiate a lucrative sale of BALR Corporation to my old company Whittman-Hart. After the merger was completed, I accepted a position with the new organization (renamed MarchFirst) as a senior partner/mentor in the Chicago office.

RON RICE

As the 14th employee of the original holding company, it was very gratifying to see the company grow to over 10,000 consultants in 46 cities and several countries. We were regarded as the largest Internet technical consulting firm in the world during the dot-com explosion of the late '90s.

It has been an honor to work with some of the brightest technology and business professionals in the technical consulting field. Together we served many of the world's largest organizations across many diverse platforms and industries. Combined revenues for projects and organizations under my leadership exceeded over a half a billion dollars. These included client technology projects, acquisitions and mergers, key man planning and placement, and strategic vendor alliances.

In July of 2001, I accepted an early retirement package from the company to pursue my interest in public speaking, venture capital, and finishing a book on building professional relationships.

I continue to stay active as an advisor/investor in several start-up organizations as well as several charitable boards across the country promoting pro-family programs and initiatives.

Erin and I spend many miles traveling this awesome country by either boat or motor home. We look forward to spoiling our grandchildren and continuing to make a professional and spiritual impact wherever and whenever possible.

I can be reached by e-mail at ricepapa@aol.com.

That's my bio.

Blowing your own horn a little is fine in a résumé. You should feel good about yourself when you read it. You don't have to be a Fortune 500 CEO to feel good about what you've accomplished.

Once you have your résumé completed, take a serious look at what you need to do for the future. Perhaps you need some more education, or need to add a skill or two. Take a few courses or seminars, and then add them to your résumé. Maybe you always wanted to learn another language? There are classes, self-paced tapes, and hundreds of books to help you accomplish any educational goal. You just need to get off your butt and make it happen.

If your job experience is a little light, you could seek a promotion or transfer within your current company to gain more experience. Your employer may have an apprentice program that will allow you to train, and then change career paths.

Building Relationships That Last A Lifetime

Regardless of where you are professionally or personally, a résumé is just like a mirror. It reflects what your doing, what you have done, and most importantly . . . what you can do! Always keep in mind just how special you are. You should see it in the mirror and in your résumé. You are God's work in progress even if you're eighty-five!

You are alive in the greatest century humankind has ever known, with opportunities around every corner. What you should see in the mirror every day is a marvel of the universe. Never sell yourself short. You can do or be anything, but it must start with what you see in the mirror, and that vision must be positive.

19.

Skill 4: Healthy and Wealthy

There are two things in life that you cannot get back once they are gone. The first is your time, and the second is your health. We talked in earlier chapters about wasting time and the importance of organization. Now let's talk about your health.

Healthy

There are three simple things that every human being can do to increase their chances of living a long and healthy life. We all know them, but few of us take them seriously. Just to refresh your memory they are a good diet, regular exercise, and a yearly physical.

A Good Diet

Americans eat too much. Too many of us are overweight. Too much fat in our diets, poor choices with carbohydrates, and sugar, sugar everywhere shortens our lives. A healthy corrective would be author Michael Pollan's advice: "Eat [real] food. Not too much. Mostly plants."[2] We need to use our heads when it comes to diet. Heart disease, diabetes, and high blood pressure are all on the rise because of diet choices. Smoking is just plain dumb, but there are still too many who do it, and we wonder why we have so much cancer. Look what we are doing to ourselves!

My father had triple bypass surgery some time ago. I spent a week in the cardiac ICU watching my dad recover from major surgery. While I was visiting, the cardiologist was making his rounds. We struck up a conversation about smoking the occasional cigar, the two-martini lunch, and the cost of that lifestyle. I will never forget what he said.

"There are forty-five beds in this ICU. Every one of these patients has two things in common. They were all overweight, and they all smoked sometime in their lives."

If you smoke, stop. If you are overweight, you need to get rid of those extra pounds ASAP. Get some support from family and friends. Your life depends on it! Remember, once it's gone . . . it's gone.

Regular Exercise

Once we get the okay from our doctor, a simple brisk walk thirty minutes a day will do the trick for most of us when it comes to exercise. You don't need a gym membership, a weight machine, or other special equipment to keep a decent level of physical fitness. Walking is a great conditioner. Start small and increase your distance, time, and terrain as you get stronger. Add a little weight in each hand (a can of corn) and you get a great upper body workout as you walk.

If you want to look like Arnold Schwarzenegger, you'll have to work much harder and longer to achieve that kind of result, but anyone can do it if they have the discipline to do the work and follow the strict diet.

I'm tired of hearing people and programs talk about a miracle system to stay in shape. Take this pill, this diet, this program and the pounds will melt away. Bullpucky! If you want to look like Michael Phelps you have to eat and work like Michael Phelps. There are no shortcuts to a world-class body. Even steroids, and a great plastic surgeon, cannot replace a ton of hours in the gym and a well-planned diet. No discipline, no centerfold body. Sorry.

A Yearly Physical

Even with a good diet and exercise, things can still go wrong with our bodies. That's why we need a good check-up at least once a year. Just like the maintenance we do for our cars, a yearly physical keeps us in the pink and running well. Should we have a problem, early detection can almost guarantee recovery.

Unfortunately, many of us do not get the check-up we need, and a silent killer slowly steals our life without any symptoms or problems until it's too late. Remember, modern medicine can fix just about any problem if physicians catch it early, but the most commonly cured problem will kill you if left undetected long enough.

So I give myself a birthday present every year—a complete physical. There are far more pleasant things to do on your birthday than make a trip to the doctor's office, but none more important. I also see the eye doctor and the dentist for the same reason.

There are some great books on the subject of health. I love the You series books by Dr. Oz, who has his own afternoon television network program. His straightforward approach to good nutrition and exercise is as easy as it gets, so anyone can do it with a little discipline and some self-control.

Wealthy

Do you know what the difference is between a rich man and a poor man? The answer is interest. A poor man pays it, and a rich man receives it.

The average American couple will spend over $300,000 in interest in their lifetimes. That three hundred grand would make a nice retirement nest egg if it were invested in an IRA, but it was lost to the interest trap.

America has been sold a bill of goods when it comes to buying things on time. The lie that the American public has been sold on is the notion that they can have anything they want as long as they can make the monthly payments. It's not what you can afford, it's what you can afford a month that is the great American tragedy promoted by the media and even our government.

This lifestyle has been promoted and encouraged by people who make a living on interest, and they love the suckers who spend their entire lives paying off debt. Just a few years ago, our country was in the middle of the worst financial crisis since the Great Depression, and all because of bad debt. In October 2008, the United States Congress bailed out the financial industry to the tune of $700 billion. The need for this bail out was too much borrowing/lending and not enough cash.

For the last several years, people could get mortgages with ridiculous terms. No money down, super low adjustable rates, and unqualified borrowers with terrible credit or too much payment for their incomes. This was a recipe for disaster. Multiply that times a million or two, and you have an entire industry of worthless debt that will never be repaid. The homeowner loses their home, the greedy banks go broke, and the taxpayers are left holding the bag!

Even if you own your home, your stocks, bonds, and other assets all have taken a hit as the economy has slumped under the failure of the financial system, and none of it needed to happen. An entire generation is on the government "stimulus" plan. These cleaver bits of legislation tie free people to their mother-government for life. It is sad, and against every idea our founding fathers ever imagined for our country. Yet every year our government grows larger and larger, taking care of more and more of its citizens. Sounds a lot like communism and less like a democracy, and that's scary.

Borrowing is dangerous. There are good reasons to borrow money, but the terms, conditions, and long-term plan must be understood and followed. Any loan where terms change as a market moves is simply a bad decision, because no one knows the direction of the future market. Agreeing to interest rates that "adjust" is gambling, because no one can predict where interest rates will go in a free market economy. So your financial future rests on a market that is always changing.

For many Americans, their homes are their largest investment. Why risk your largest asset with an adjustable interest rate mortgage? The short-term interest savings are not worth the risk of a large payment increase when rates adjust. Your paycheck does not change with the rise and fall of interest rates, so how can your largest payment? Thousands who took the interest-rate gamble back in 2008 lost their homes. Now where are they?

Wealthy is a state of mind and a little common sense. Here are four rules to follow when it comes to your finances. They are simple, easy to remember, and powerful life-changers.

Wealth Rule #1: Never borrow money to purchase something that goes down in value

We should not borrow to buy items that depreciate in value. That includes things like cars, furniture, vacations, and clothes. In fact, I can think of only two things you should ever invest in with borrowed money: *your home* and *your education*. That's it. Everything else will keep you from achieving financial independence.

If you borrow money for education or a home, make sure your loan terms are fixed for the entire length of the loan. Forget any program where your payments "adjust." Your monthly payments should *never* change. In fact, you should have the ability to pay the loan off early with no penalty. Good terms must be part of your loan. Shop around and get several loan offers before you make your final decision. Borrowing money for any other reason will keep you poor.

The most common interest mistake is buying a new car on payments. Read the fine print of a finance contract, and you will see that the new car didn't cost you $25,000. If you pay it off over five years it really cost you $35,000! Even if you get rid of the car in two years, you still took a bath because of interest and depreciation.

One of the largest financial bondage games in the world today is the credit card. Credit cards themselves are actually good financial instruments when they are used correctly. You get an itemized list of all your charges each month, and many credit card companies also give you a year-end statement of all charges by category just in time for tax season. This is a powerful tool for tracking your expenses.

Credit cards become a problem when they are used to finance purchases. Most credit cards allow you to make minimum payments. Unfortunately, these payments are usually just the interest and no principal. Mix in a super-high interest rate, and you have an equation for disaster. This credit card situation has gotten so bad, that an entire industry has sprung up specializing in helping people get out of credit card debt. I saw one commercial looking for people with at least $10,000 in credit card debt as a minimum!

Interest on purchases that go down in value will keep most people working their entire lives just to pay back debt. That is a shame, because a little education and a bit of self-control would have made all the difference.

I love using my credit card to buy things. I get airline miles and all kinds of other goodies for using my card. I pay my bill in full each month at exactly midnight of the due date. I get thirty days of free money, and first-class airline tickets anytime I wish to fly, and all for free! I even tried to buy a car once with my credit card. I could have earned an extra thirty-five thousand flyer miles if the dealership would have allowed it. You can charge anything you want, just make sure you have the money ready in thirty days to pay off your purchases. Interest-free borrowing is great. Credit card debt is not!

How can credit card companies afford to give me free vacations? They have millions of people paying interest every month by paying the minimum payments. These accounts make billions for the credit card companies, so they don't mind sending me on vacation for free. You have every right to get free goodies too. Do you pay interest, or does interest pay you? The choice is yours.

So how do we live without making interest payments?

Wealth Rule #2: Cash is king

If you want to buy something, buy it with cash. If the item is a large purchase, get a picture of the item, place it where you see it every day, and save the money to buy it. You will enjoy it even more when you saved for it and paid cash verses running out and making an emotional decision with a credit card.

Cars are terrible investments. Unless you drive a 1966 Corvette, your vehicle is going down in value so fast it would astound you. If you buy or lease a new car, you've lost thousands of dollars as soon as you leave the showroom. Yet thousands of people do it every day.

I love the car commercials. They show a cool car on the screen with all the bells and whistles. They tell the viewer that they can *drive* this car for only $299 per month. That's right, you can drive that car for $299 per month, but you do not own anything. The car company's finance division owns the car, and they own you for five years or longer. You don't own a thing until that last payment is made.

I don't mean to pick on the car companies of America. It's not their fault that most people think poor. Want a new car? Walk in with cash and negotiate your tail off. Don't have the cash? Check out the used car market. You pay half the price because someone else took the depreciation loss. Interest is the key. Don't let your short-term desires invite interest in your life. Once he moves in, he's a tough houseguest to get rid of.

Buying a Home (Mortgage)

There is, however, such a thing as "good interest." Buying a home instead of renting is a great reason to borrow money. Mortgage interest is deductible from your taxes, and you are building equity with every monthly payment as your house goes up in value. Houses usually go up in value unless you buy in high-risk areas or in swampland. Most people can select a home in a good neighborhood without too much trouble. A home in this environment is one of the best investments you will ever make.

Work to pay it off early if possible, and don't fall for the line about taking out a home equity loan—it's a scam. The home equity interest rate is far less than a credit card, but it is still interest, and interest robs wealth. Be careful to negotiate your home purchase price, mortgage rate, bank fees, and other charges aggressively. If you've protected your credit score, you're a valuable customer to the mortgage and banking industry. Make them earn your business with a great rate and low or no fees. Everything is negotiable in a real-estate transaction. Check out your local library for some good books on buying a house and negotiating with a mortgage company. Knowledge is power. What you don't know will cost you dough!

Paying for an Education (Student Loan)

The second type of "good interest" is a student loan for education. I said education, and not a new car, trip to Italy, or other nondegree activities using student loan money. There are so many programs available today for a college education that you would be hard-pressed to find a student who could not get some financing for college. The problem is that most people don't try, or give up too quickly.

One of my favorite questions to college administrators is, why the high cost of tuition, books, and living expenses at most colleges? You would be amazed by the difference in cost of a basic Algebra class from college to college even though they are teaching the same material. Since costs vary wildly across the country, it pays to shop around. Start thinking about college when your student enters high school. A little research each year will keep you from scrambling and making a bad choice six months before they enter college.

Once you've found the perfect college for you or your student, spend quality time with the financial aid office. Regardless of your income, background, or credit score, there are thousands of grants, scholarships, and financial aid programs available. Many do not require anything more than the application. Many of these programs go unused because no one applies for them. Don't leave that money on the table. If you have the desire to better yourself, college is great place to start. The excuse that you can't afford it does not hold water anymore. It just takes some research to find the cash.

If you use student loans to finance your education, make sure you pay them off as soon as possible. This accomplishes two important goals for your future. First, you get interest out of your life as soon as possible. Even though this is good interest, it's still interest! Second, you establish a good credit history right out of school.

When to Get a Credit Card

Let me take a quick moment for my younger readers who are toying with credit cards. Don't get a credit card just to establish credit. That's playing

Russian roulette just to learn to shoot a gun! Start with a simple checking and savings account that pays you interest on every penny you deposit. I know rates are terribly low, but something is better than nothing and anything is certainly better than paying interest. Pay your bills on time, build up a good savings account with your local bank or credit union, and your credit score will naturally rise.

When you are ready to use a credit card properly, then get one. When you do, make sure you pay the entire balance every month with no exceptions. If you do not have the money in the bank, then don't make the purchase with a credit card.

Good financial control and education come first, credit card second, and financial freedom for life. When our finances are in order, we can do a better job at building relationships that last a lifetime. This is true because we take one more distraction out of our lives when we get control of interest and money in general.

Wealth Rule #3: Save $25 per week for life

Many people at my seminars tell me that they are going to start saving next year after they pay off their student loans, credit cards, and a few other personal loans. This is just one more excuse to poverty.

It takes a few dollars a week in a solid savings investment account to be financially secure. Unfortunately, young people are not taught that in high school or college, and get started too late in life. They are forced to spend their entire working lives playing catch up, or they can never stop working.

Take your average high school graduate who saves just $25 per week. You can't buy one tank of gasoline for $25, that's less than $5 per day! Anyone can come up with five bucks! Five bucks adds up to $1,200 per year.

Saving $5 a day over a period of thirty years gets real exciting. By the time you are forty-eight years old, you will have amassed a small fortune. While you invested just $25 per week, the money at year thirty, diversified into some blue-chip stocks and bonds, would be in the millions!

Wealth Rule #4: Give

When you start earning a living, one of the most powerful wealth lessons is giving. Wealth, like relationships, is not about us. It's about the other guy. As you get a handle on your finances by eliminating bad interest, paying cash, and saving regularly, you need only one more rule in your life to experience wealth. Many people give a certain percentage of their incomes to charity. I'm not concerned how much you give, I just want you to give.

The reason why giving is so powerful is deep inside each one of us. We all were helped by someone sometime in our lives. A parent, friend, coach, or teacher made a difference. We can make a difference in someone's life as well by giving. Your money helps feed people, cure diseases, educate, house, clothe, and rescue someone else. Just like someone rescued you. Wonderful things will happen to your finances when you give. Always make your gifts in secret. Giving is a personal thing between you and yourself.

One of the true joys of being financially successful is helping others. The houses, cars, boats, planes, and bank accounts will not bring satisfaction. Giving will.

20.

Skill 5: Balance

What are your plans for this weekend? Hopefully, you have scheduled something. Even if you're scheduled event is reading a good book or lounging in the backyard. It was scheduled.

My seminars convince most people of the need to organize their work day. It makes sense professionally and financially. My toughest challenge as a trainer and coach is to get people fired up about scheduling their weekends, vacations, and free time.

Skill #5 is about leading a balanced life.

Plan Your Weekends

Too many of us gain our identities from what we do instead of who we are. Using the Big Three (see chapter 16 on the skill of organization), we should take charge of our weekends just as thoroughly as we take care of Mondays. Planning our days off is just as important as our work week. Is your weekend for family time? Great! What family activities do you have planned for next weekend? Get the kids involved in planning early and often. You'd be amazed what is really important to them.

Even if you are a single person, planning for the weekend is important to you also. Get involved in a hobby, volunteer work, a sports club or team, art class, photography, or one or more of a hundred other possibilities. Don't let free time become dead time.

RON RICE

As an employer, I used to encourage my people to attack their weekends. I was also a huge fan of comp time (allowing people time off instead of pay for overtime). If your position allows for you to work a longer day and take a three-day weekend, do it. The fruits of a job well done are free time and a little cash to have some fun. "You can't take it with you" is an old saying that is so true about free time.

I was fortunate enough to retire early. There is not a single day that goes by that has me wishing to return to work. People always ask me, how does a huge type A personality stay busy in retirement? Easy. I plan my days just as aggressively in retirement as I did while running a company.

My wife and I love to travel. We've owned a motor home for many years and enjoy traveling around this great country of ours. We usually take friends or family with us on our adventures. Over the last three years, we have been on a mission to see all of the national parks. We are set for our seventh trip to visit the northeastern United States. This trip will include stops in Ohio, New York, Maine, Rhode Island, Virginia, and Kentucky. This trip will run under three thousand miles. When we reach a national park, we get our passport book stamped. Our goal is to get all fifty-six national park stamps.

I also ride a Harley. I've been across this country from shore to shore three times. I rode around Lake Michigan one summer not long ago. Awesome sunsets!

Here is a partial list of things we have planned in the coming years:

Spend the summer in Alaska by motor home
Cruise our boat around the Great Circle route
Attend the 2016 Summer Olympics in Rio de Janeiro, Brazil
Take every grandchild and their parents to Disney World at least once
Attend a Daytona 500
Attend a Kentucky Derby
Attend at least one Super Bowl

I usually start working on a trip or event at least one year in advance. Retirement doesn't mean we stop planning or living. Time is time, and health is health; what we do with what we have honors the One who gave it to us.

Try not to waste a day. They are too precious.

Having a well-organized weekend refreshes the body and soul. Work becomes more challenging and rewarding when you take the time to recharge those batteries.

Building Relationships That Last A Lifetime

Don't misunderstand me, scheduling a quiet weekend with nothing but rest and relaxation is a great way to spend time, but I still want it scheduled in advance. *Manage your time, or it will manage you!*

Television often portrays the run-down executive who turns to the camera and says, "Boy, do I need a vacation." The reason this poor fellow looks so run-down is poor time management. If his life was more organized and balanced, he'd have a vacation every weekend!

Taking Work Home

There are many people who insist on taking work home and have a fully functional office in their house. This can be a very dangerous situation if not managed properly. Work is work, and home is home. Even if you work out of your home, keep those boundaries clear and understood.

I had a standing rule when it came to business telephone calls at home. You could call me at home if the issue was your life or death. Otherwise, we can deal with the crisis first thing in the morning at the office. The same held true for my weekends. Life and death only, or let it wait until Monday.

In twenty-five years, there never was a business problem that needed my attention on a Saturday. I never asked a client for their home phone number, nor did I ever give my home phone number to a client. What business problem could I possibly solve or create with a home phone number that could not wait till morning?

When I talk with professionals from many different organizations, I find that those people who work six or seven days a week have something in common. They are either poor delegators of work or they are poor organizers of their own desk. Both are problems and shorten both your professional career and your personal life. I guarantee that I could spend a week with the workaholic and get their activities and responsibilities in order and organized.

Other than the occasional bolt-of-lightning problem or opportunity, there is no position that requires more than forty hours per week. If the position does require more than forty hours, it is really two positions cleverly disguised as one. Hire another sharp person for the additional forty hours of work, and then go home and spend some time with your family.

Many workaholics love what they do too much and for the wrong reasons. Long hours keep them from home by design. A rough marriage, troubled kids, or other family or personal relationships are too painful for our sixty-hour-a-week executive, so they keep at work where things are easier to control. Eventually, the real trouble can no longer be ignored, and both the career and the family relationships are threatened.

If you are a professional who spends too much time at work, be honest with yourself about what you are really doing. Address what's really taking so much time; talk with a friend or professional counselor. Any problem can be fixed given honesty, time, and work.

Balance in you daily life allows rest, recharge, and rejuvenation. With a fresh outlook on life, relationships look different also. We see clearly when we are rested and recharged. Without balance, we lose both our professional and personal well-being. Fatigue, disease, and personal conflict can all start with burnout. Burnout comes from a lack of balance.

A balanced life requires all of us to work. No work causes just as many problems as too much work. Welfare, overindulgent parents, and a misguided society have created a whole class of people who are robbed of balance by not knowing a good day's work. Since these poor individuals do not work, they do not experience the pride, financial rewards, and professional relationships we all need for a healthy existence.

Society does not help a struggling person with an aid check. That is only a band-aid placed on a major wound. If the state is really interested in helping someone down on their luck, forget the cash, train them in a skill that is needed in the marketplace, and help them get a good job. Sending someone who does not work a check every month guarantees their captivity. Unfortunately, I think many people in power want to keep people this way so they can be controlled and manipulated.

God does not tell us how many days we get on this earth, so we need to make each day count. Relationships that last a lifetime require a balanced life. Balancing our life is a daily process that we can win. Work to live . . . Never live to work!

21

Skill 6: Give Back

The skill of giving is probably the most personally rewarding of all the skills. Being able to help, teach, share, and carry someone else's burdens is a powerful way to build relationships. Songs, poems, works of art, and great novels have filled the ages of history talking about giving and sharing yourself with others.

Giving is more than money. It's also your time and your talents and you as a human being. The easiest thing to do is write a check. That's a great start, but you have so much more to offer to a hurting world. They need your relationship right now.

There is so much need and so few people interested in sharing just a little of their fortune. I believe America could eradicate just about every inch of poverty in our country if everyone would just give a little time, talent, and treasure. Just a small portion from everyone would change the world.

If every church, synagogue, and temple would adopt just one orphan per congregation, there would be no orphans. Adopting a child by a single family is a large commitment, but sharing that commitment with one hundred families would be no problem at all. Most churches could take an entire family.

The same would hold true for hunger, job training, housing, and troubled homes. It's a simple matter of organization, planning, and recruiting others to join in. No one has to tackle the project by themselves. Let's build a few relationships and get things rolling.

Most people would love to share, but they just sit on the sidelines watching others. If you are one of the people doing something, grab a friend or neighbor next time. I promise you they are just waiting for you to nudge them into the pool, and they will never get out! Events sponsored by the March of Dimes, Special Olympics, and the American Cancer Society are really addicting. Once you get connected and start those relationships, the connection usually lasts a lifetime, and people get help in the process.

Counting on the state or federal government to solve all of society's problems is not only crazy, it's lazy. These people in need are our neighbors. They are our responsibility. Did you know our founding fathers designed the federal government for only two functions? First, to provide for the national defense, and second to regulate trade between the states. That's it. Everything else should be handled at the local, county, and state levels.

Government and its programs are involved in everything. People expect our elected officials to solve every problem we have from educating our children to financing our homes. I'd like the federal government to be 200 percent smaller and let me and my neighbors run our community without interference from some far-off bureaucracy that is too big to solve anything other than getting reelected. Volunteers are the only way to solve all the ailments of society, and we all need to get involved.

Interesting things will happen in your life when you unleash the power of giving. It is contagious. It's a blast being Santa or dropping off free turkeys on Thanksgiving or being a Little League coach even when you do not have a son or daughter on the team. Those of you who do these things on a regular basis know how much more you get back than you ever give.

If you are one of those givers, thank you for your service. Your gift makes the world a better place. The relationships you build when you give are just one of the many blessings you receive. If you have never tried giving back, jump in and try it. You don't have to build a wing on a hospital to make a difference. Just make yourself available, and watch what happens.

The relationships you will make in giving back will change you life. Don't miss them.

22.

Skill 7: Pass It On

Skill # 7 is the reason for this book. I wanted to pass this book on to you.

After twenty-five years of professional relationship building, and eight years as a retired investor/advisor, this book is another way for me to pass on what I know to thousands of people. By sharing this knowledge, I sharpen my own skills as a relationship builder.

When you pass on what you know, you make that material a part of your inner self. Sharing knowledge, skill, or technique with someone else refines your knowledge like fire cures iron. The more you share, the stronger your skill becomes. If you keep what you know to yourself, the opposite will happen and you will slowly lose the edge. Burnout and fatigue will be your constant companions until you have trouble doing anything productive. By mentoring, training, or coaching others, you cement the ideas you teach into your own daily life. The best way to improve your technique in any activity is to teach it to someone else.

My sales career was never stronger or more productive than when I was working with a new salesperson or team. As I taught them the ins and outs of the business, I was constantly reviewing my own application of the materials. Most of my improvements, changes, and planning were developed while working with others.

Want to see if your skills and techniques are really on track? Teach them to someone else and watch the result. If your student seems out of sync or going in the wrong direction, your ideas, strategies, and techniques may need a little overhaul. No matter how skilled or exciting you and your position are, we all get tired and sloppy sometimes. One of the best ways to avoid this problem is by passing your experience on to someone else. There is something about working with a new person that recharges the mind. I've never seen this practice fail professionally or personally.

By keeping our skill and knowledge to ourselves, we limit our growth. The free exchange of ideas is a powerful opportunity to teach and to learn. To start this exchange we must be willing to ask questions, seek advice, and listen more than we speak. This activity sounds a little like building relationships.

When we reach out to establish a relationship with anyone, we have the opportunity to share our knowledge and experience. The give-and-take of getting to know someone is a fantastic source of learning if we will only open up our ears. The exchange of skills and ideas recharges our own careers as we pass on our experiences to someone else.

Want to make something yours forever? Pass it on. Want to guarantee you'll lose it? Keep it to yourself. To stay sharp your entire life, pass on what you know on a regular basis.

೮೩ ೮೩

There you have the seven skills that everyone needs to develop if they want to maximize their relationships and enjoy an abundant life. I've met many successful people in my life, and tried to learn something from each one. These skills are lessons learned from such individuals.

Like all life-changing techniques, these skills will take time to learn and apply in your life. Start with one and make it your own. Once you have incorporated into your daily routine, add another skill and do the same. You will begin to notice a change in how you think, act, and treat others.

When I run a seminar, I tell the attendees that I do not plan on leaving them as I found them. I want to convince them to change. These seven skills are the heart of what I talk about. They have application in the lives of CEOs as well as high school students.

The knowledge is now yours, but it is your application of it that changes lives.

23.

Ron's Rules

Over the years, I've always enjoyed a good motivational line or two. The following are some of my own creations. I think Benjamin Franklin might smile if he were to read a few of my maxims. I've listed the chapter where this idea is developed.

1. Trust must always come before any request.
   (Seven touches to build trust, from chapter 6.)
2. Great products and services are always created by the needs of the customer and never from the mind of the supplier.
   (Know your customer, from chapter 11.)
3. Knowledge without application is simply trivia.
   (Application and discipline, from chapter 9.)
4. Any thought or inspiration not written down will be quickly lost forever. *(Organization and your personal business journal, from chapter 16; also see chapter 5.)*
5. The difference between a rich man and a poor man is interest. A rich man receives it . . . and a poor man pays it.
   (Healthy and wealthy, from chapter 19.)
6. What you do not know about your health will eventually kill you. *(Healthy and wealthy, from chapter 19.)*
7. A person cannot achieve anything their mind cannot see.
   (Positive self-image, from chapter 18.)
8. A person's self-worth should come from who they are and never from what they do. (Balance, from chapter 20.)
9. Your fields must be far larger than the harvest you expect.
   (The art of farming, from chapter 4.)
10. True mastering of any skill comes only when that skill is successfully taught to someone else. *(Pass it on, from chapter 22)*
11. What matters most are the relationships you developed and embraced during your life. Those relationships will carry a valuable piece of you long after your death. *(The entire purpose of this book.)*

Conclusion

America . . . Still the Land of Opportunity

Thank you for taking the time to read this book. I hope you have gleaned a few gems from its pages that you can apply in your life.

America is still the greatest experiment in opportunity ever created on this planet. Even though we still trip and stumble to make this country the land of opportunity for everyone who lives here, we still have the best deal going. Where in the world could a college dropout (a mere six weeks) become a multimillionaire by the age of forty? It happens every day in America. Somewhere someone is willing to chase a dream. Taking a leap of faith mixed with a little good timing and voilà—a whole new company and industry is born.

As Americans, we all have so much to be thankful for. Where else on earth can anyone's dreams and ambitions be limited only by the size of their heart? It does not matter who your family is, where they came from, or the government connections you have. There are still companies in America who will take a hardworking person with no education and train them, pay them to go to school, and promote them up through the ranks limited only by their own drive and discipline. One of them was my largest client. This well-known restaurant chain has actually taken people with no education and over a period of years, made them a store-owning millionaire. What a great company.

Dreams require work, and large dreams require large amounts of it. Unfortunately, too many of us have been sold a bill of goods. Our dreams are crushed by knuckleheads who are afraid to try themselves, so they must stand in the way of someone else or stand on the sidelines and ridicule those competing in the game of life. Don't let someone tell you it can't be done. If you are the knucklehead holding others back, take a time-out and review your criticism. Being a very negative and impatient person does not change behavior or results. Constructive suggestion should be the goal of all coaches and mentors even though giving it (not to mention receiving it) can be very difficult now and then.

RON RICE

During my seminars, I ask my audience about my chances to win an Olympic gold medal in the 100-meter dash. I talk in great detail about my positive vision of standing on the medal platform with the national anthem playing in the background. My technique of running the hundred meters, strategy, positioning, and even mental preparation are all outlined in great detail. At the end of my game-plan description, I ask the audience by a show of hands, who thinks I can actually win the gold medal?

No one ever raises their hand.

After my poor showing in the confidence pole, I query the audience why they don't think my chances are very good. The typical answer is my level of conditioning based on my physical appearance. Turning fifty this year, I don't look that bad, but it's easy to see that at six foot two, 240 pounds, I do not look like a world-class sprinter, so the audience response has merit. I take all of the reasons the audience thinks my victory is impossible and write them on the whiteboard. What do all these reason have in common? Every negative response to my victory is based on my lack of discipline as a sprinter.

To achieve great things in life, we must have the discipline to do the mundane, simple, and boring things every day to be successful. Whether we are chasing Olympic gold or starting our own business, the discipline of doing the job every day based on a plan makes all the difference.

There are thousands of people with great ideas and large dreams. Why do so many fail to see them through? There are many reasons, but they all come back to discipline. Do we want to have a body like Chuck Norris or Christie Brinkley? If the answer is yes, how much time and work are you willing to spend in the gym? What foods do you push away? What sacrifices are you willing to make to have a body that stops time?

Most of us are not willing to pay the price, yet we dream of the result, or tear down the person who accomplishes the goal. We make excuses such as "She was born with good genes" or "He must have a great plastic surgeon," anything to justify our jealousy and bitterness. Anyone can have a well-toned, muscular and fit body. It just takes discipline and effort, and no excuses. If it is important to you, then pay the price. If it isn't, don't begrudge someone who did the work and got the result. They earned it!

The same is true with financial success. Unless you win the lottery or have a rich uncle who dies and leaves you a bundle, you will have to work long, hard, and smart hours to achieve that house on the hill. You have just as much right and intelligence as the millionaire next door. Are you willing to do what it takes to get there? If your answer is yes, best of success to you as you start your journey. Don't forget to enjoy the ride on your way to your dreams. If your answer is no, that's okay, but be happy with your lot in life. Having things doesn't make you happy. It's what's inside that brings happiness and not what you drive.

It's been one of the great pleasures of my life to meet hundreds of people from all walks of society. I've met the richest people in America, and even spent some time with some of the poorest. Every person has something to offer, and we need to build relationships with many different types of people to enrich our lives and allow us to serve others. Relationships that last a lifetime are important to everyone. Whether you are a giant of industry or a hardworking mother raising well-adjusted kids, we all need relationships. (Thank you, moms!) It truly is who you know that makes life exciting.

Since this is serious business, we need to work smart to develop our relationships at all levels. From our friends to our Maker, opportunities abound to change lives and to have our lives changed. Today offers you the chance to change your life right now. Start taking notes, taking notice, and taking charge of your life. It's never too late to make a positive change.

A wise man once said, "The world steps aside for a man who knows where he's going." I hope this book solidified what you already knew, challenged you on some ideas you may have considered before, and motivated you to action. Go do something great. Take a few people with you, and change the world one relationship at a time for a lifetime.

Footnotes

[1] "Bell System Advertisements—Human Desire to Communicate with Others," Bell System Memorial, The Porticus Centre, Beatrice, accessed February 22, 2012, http://www.porticus.org/bell/bellsystem_ads-1.html; Nancy Friedman, "Does 'Reach Out' Overreach?" October 4, 2011, Vocabulary.com blog, http://www.vocabulary.com/articles/candlepwr/2991/.

[2] Michael Pollen, In Defense of Food: An Eater's Manifesto (New York: Penguin Press, 2008), 1.

Made in the USA
San Bernardino, CA
28 March 2014